Cindy Lora-Renard

Foreword by Michael J Tamura

THE BUSINESS OF FORGIVENESS

Healing Yourself Through the
Practice of *A Course in Miracles*

"I could count on one hand the number of teachers of the modern spiritual masterpiece, A Course in Miracles, who absolutely refuse to compromise on its non-dualistic, radical message. Cindy Lora-Renard is one of them, and that alone would be enough for me to recommend this book. But with The Business of Forgiveness: Healing Yourself Through the Practice of A Course in Miracles, Cindy not only sticks to the truth, she fearlessly handles many topics that most teachers don't even want to go near. If you peruse the table of contents, you'll immediately start to see what I mean. I'm not merely in love with Cindy, I'm honored to have her as a teaching partner. I sincerely believe that after you've read this book you may find yourself on a spiritual path that has been miraculously accelerated."

— **Gary R. Renard**, the best-selling
   author of The Disappearance of the Universe

"If I had to describe this book in 10 words, I would choose Joan of Arc's statement: 'All battles are first won or lost in the mind.' Cindy's second book is an odyssey of human contemporary crises, with one simple and effective solution for despair and disconnection. Inspired by the teachings of Jesus from A Course in Miracles, Cindy, uncompromisingly, articulates the principles of non-dualistic thinking and perception. She, gently and lovingly (and anyone who gets to meet Cindy in person would agree she is a living example of gentleness) invites us to "choose again" an alternative perspective that cannot but help us awaken from the dream of separation to the true home we've never left."

— **Gabriela Ilie, Ph.D.**, professor in community health
   and epidemiology at Dalhousie University,
   Faculty of Medicine, Halifax, Nova Scotia

Cindy Lora-Renard

Foreword by Michael J Tamura

THE BUSINESS OF
FORGIVENESS

Healing Yourself Through the
Practice of *A Course in Miracles*

To my dear sweet husband, Gary R. Renard
May the blessing of truth dawn upon our minds,
where only joy and eternal peace abide.
Love forever and forever in love, Cindy

We came from God…
We've never left God…
So we're going nowhere.

Cindy Lora-Renard

CONTENTS

FOREWORD

I was given a choice, when I died the first time.

Five divine beings welcomed me home. They congratulated me, saying I had fulfilled my purpose, far beyond what I had originally agreed to do. I was done with my earthly life and was not required to return to it. Instead, I was free to choose: continue my work in Spirit with the masters or re-up for another tour of duty in the world. I had no desires either way. What was God's Will?

I knew the answer instantly: I was to make the choice. So, being in the presence of such fully awakened masters, I chose to ask them for their wisdom. What would serve the greater benefit for all who were concerned: for me to continue in Spirit or to return to the dream we call the world? They answered in complete unison: A far greater benefit would be served for all concerned if I returned to my earthly life.

So, I told them, "Send me back."

When I returned here to this world, it was a complete rebirth. So it was also when I returned the second time. I've died five times in all during my current incarnation. Each death and each return was a completely different experience. When I returned for the third time, however, it was not a re-birth—it was the beginning of resurrection.

Contrary to popular belief, resurrection has nothing to do with raising dead bodies from their graves—or bringing anyone back from physical death to the earthly life. It has to do instead with fully waking ourselves up from the dream of being a body. It's a lot more like recovery—not from alcohol and drugs—but from our addiction to any and all illusions. We're here to kick our habit of playing this video game as if it's our true reality. We call it living-in-this-world. But, reality? <Spoiler Alert!> It's not. If we are to free ourselves from our dependency on illusions, we have to get down to the business of forgiveness.

This remarkable book you now hold in your hands offers you the wise guidance and the impeccable tools to help you find your way back to your true home. I can say that it is truly heaven sent: Everything in it, I have experienced in my sojourns beyond time and space in heaven. It shows you, step-by-step, how to go about your business of forgiving. You will discover that, in the end, all healing comes down to forgiving; so why not get in the express lane and start with forgiveness now?

Cindy Lora-Renard certainly did. She's the angel who wrote this book. She rolled up her mental sleeves and got down to the business of forgiveness. All that she's experienced along the way is nothing short of miraculous—and, now, she's mapped it out for you in this book, so with practice, you, too, can learn to heal yourself and live more of the miracle of the limitless. By offering you this book, she's giving you the gift of making a new choice for yourself. This choice, however, is not between two equally limited options like right and wrong, good and bad, male and female, black and white, Democrat and Republican, or religious and not religious. The choice Cindy offers is between what truly is and what merely appears to be; between the eternal and the temporal; between God's Grace and the ego's tyranny. One will lead you to healing, the other to suffering. We each have the freedom to choose.

If we weren't suffering in some way, we wouldn't need healing, would we? Whether we are conscious of it or not, healing is what we all seek, in some form, when we are suffering, because we seek to restore ourselves to the experience of wholeness. We intuitively know that our suffering somehow comes from us being divided within ourselves, separate from the whole, isolated. We know our suffering isn't true, we know there has to be a healthy, happy version of ourselves somewhere.

So, we often find ourselves in a Catch-22 when we experience invalidation: We desperately want to be whole again, yet, we isolate ourselves even more to protect ourselves and lick our wounds. How can we ever heal ourselves, however, if we isolate ourselves? And, the suffering seems never-ending.

That's why we need courageous, compassionate, and trustworthy guides to help us navigate through the labyrinth of our lives. We need the wise counsel of those who have "been there, done that" through the desert of their own experience of suffering and have somehow managed to find the oasis of healing and happiness. We may at first seek some kind of magical treatment or person to make us well and happy. Yet, in the depth of our suffering, we always eventually discover that there is no one and nothing in the world that can do it for us. That, however, doesn't sentence us to hopelessness. Rather, it is hope calling to us that we need guidance and the proper tools to find our way back to the limitless, radiant, and loving light that we are.

Speaking to you through this book, Cindy will be your courageous, compassionate, and trustworthy guide. Although her impressive academic and professional credentials can be found on her website, CV, and resume, Cindy's true credentials for writing this book can only come from having lived and continuing to live everything she shares in it. It is only through fully experiencing the truth of our life that we can distill it into wisdom.

I know Cindy Lora-Renard is a courageous soul. Any of us can talk about forgiveness, but, it takes great courage to live it every day. Courage comes from repeatedly choosing to love, rather than trying to defend ourselves against our fears. I know Cindy courageously and lovingly practices the true forgiveness that she writes about in this book, because every time I see her in person, her radiance and grace have grown exponentially, since the previous time I saw her. As a teacher, she teaches the only way that a true teacher can ever teach—by demonstration in living her own life anew each day.

When you read this book, the compassion that inspired Cindy to offer you this gift touches you. Herein, nothing is sugar-coated, because compassion always empowers; it never demeans. Yet, you will see that Cindy points you toward the truth with utmost gentleness and the torment of judgment evanesces when her compassion hugs you.

Above all, perhaps the most important attribute we seek in a guide at first, when we seek safe passage through uncharted territory to our destination, is whether that guide is worthy of our trust. Incidentally, the same could be said about a friend. As a guide on our journey of awakening, I trust Cindy implicitly to help me keep my sight on my destination. As a wonderful friend, I know she has my back. I trust Cindy that she practices trusting only the Spirit of God.

Cindy is exactly the courageous, compassionate, and trustworthy guide we need to help us find our way through the many ups-and-downs and the twists-and-turns in our lives and even more so along our spiritual path of awakening and healing; but, is Cindy really an angel? My trusty little dictionary here defines an angel as "a spiritual being believed to act as an attendant, agent, or messenger of God, conventionally represented in human form with wings and a long robe."

The Cindy I know hides her wings well, especially in public. She most likely owns a long robe or two, but I've never seen her wear one. She did, however, look simply angelic in her long white wedding dress when Raphaelle, my wife, and I officiated Gary's and her wedding. Far more importantly, she is a beautiful spiritual being, who is an attendant, agent, and messenger of God—of that, I am certain. What she has written in this book not only validates what I have experienced of the Eternal and Limitless, but also offers essential tools and practices to help you wake up to the undivided loving wholeness of Spirit.

Today, the ever-increasing turmoil and tribulations in this world demand that we keep our vision on the path paved by a fully awakened One, namely Jesus—the Voice of A Course in Miracles. And He offers us his timeless encouragement: "Be of good cheer for I have overcome the world."

Open your mind beyond its seeming limits. Learn to look and see as Spirit, and transcend the suffering in this world. Discover the true nature and purpose of forgiveness and free yourself. Be the light of the world that you are!

I invite you to read on.

Michael J Tamura   October 2020

AUTHOR'S NOTE AND ACKNOWLEDGEMENTS

Since 2005, I have been a student of the modern, spiritual masterpiece called A Course in Miracles that provides the inspiration for this book. I have been formally teaching it since 2009. I always consider myself a student of this great work, since it is clear that the Voice of A Course in Miracles, channeled through a woman named Helen Schucman in the 60's, represents a wisdom beyond time and space. The Voice makes it very clear that it is Jesus speaking through Helen since he often speaks in the first person and clarifies what he was teaching over 2000 years ago. I have often sought out wisdom from great masters throughout history, and wanted to find out how they became enlightened, so when A Course in Miracles crossed my path, I was naturally drawn to the wise, authoritative, but loving Voice of the Holy Spirit, which is what Jesus represents.

I was inspired to write a series of books that reinforce and expand on certain themes in A Course in Miracles, which I will simply call the Course from this moment on, this one being about forgiveness as taught by Jesus whose real name was Jeshua. Since most people are familiar with the name Jesus, I decided to keep it that way in my writings. This book represents the second book in my series.

As I have grown and reflected on the spiritual principles as taught in the Course, I have noticed that my world view has shifted to such a degree that I can no longer place the responsibility for any upsets I experience as coming from outside of me. This has made my life freer, fuller, and more peaceful. If I look in the mirror, and keep insisting that the reflection has to change in order for me to be happy, I am only dealing with an effect, which is not the source of change. If I want to change, I have to change the cause, which is my mind, and what is reflected will follow. This is such an easy principle in theory, but I realize it can be difficult to practice, especially when something hits the fan that is not love. This is why maintaining a sense of humor is important on the path to healing, and I have done my best to keep things somewhat light, while still addressing the deeper spiritual issues we face.

My purpose for writing this book is to help deepen and reinforce the powerful meaning of true forgiveness, like planting a seed, so that whoever is ready to water it, will help it grow with me. In the sharing of an idea, it strengthens, and starts to become a part of you, quite literally. I can't think of a better idea to share than forgiveness, especially in a world where guilt, struggle, and uncertainty, all of which are components of fear, are dominant.

Pure non-dualism, a term that will become more clear to you as we go along, and is the truth that Jesus (along with other masters in history) was teaching, is starting to emerge out of the deep waters of the unconsciously addictive dualistic world, paving the way for a new way of being, thinking, and navigating through the dream here we call life. You will see that with an open mind, and the willingness to explore, a whole new world will emerge that represents the "real" you that God created whole and perfect.

As my experience with the Course has grown, my passion for teaching and writing about it has deepened, and the process has become more meditative. The ideas are being reinforced in my own mind to such a degree that it truly brings me joy to express it with others.

I quote often from the Course throughout the book to help further reinforce and clarify certain ideas that are being expressed. References to the Course, including each chapter's introductory quotation, are noted and listed in the Endnotes in the back of the book.

My deepest gratitude goes to the Voice of the Course, whose unconditional love for us all has inspired me beyond my imagination. Also, a profound expression of thanks to the scribe of the Course, Dr. Helen Schucman, for being willing to fulfill her assignment in taking down notes from the Voice so that it could be shared with millions of people. Her colleague and co-scribe, Bill Thetford, also played a pivotal role in bringing the Course to fruition, working with Helen, and inspiring her to keep moving forward with this most beautiful and compelling document.

I want to thank my loving husband, Gary R. Renard, for always encouraging me and reminding me to laugh, and for his own powerful contribution to the Course community and the world in general, expressing the teachings of the Course, along with Arten and Pursah (the Ascended Masters who appear to Gary), in such a funny, yet impactful and unique way. I am grateful we are awakening in God together.

I further want to acknowledge my incredible family and friends for their unconditional love and support. More specifically, I thank my mother, Doris Lora, a Course student and the editor of this book. Her demonstration and understanding of the Course is inspiring, and truly appreciated. Her love and support means so much to me. I would also like to thank my father, Ron Lora, for his endless encouragement and support of my journey, always being willing to listen with an open mind, and show such a genuine interest in my path. Thank you. More love and gratitude to my sister, Jackie Lora Jones, also a student and teacher of the Course, who is truly an inspiration to me and my soul sister on the path of awakening. I would also like to give a profound thank you to my brother-in-law, Mark Jones, who so graciously lent a helping hand when needed, especially in the area of tech support. His desire to be truly helpful is admirable. I also want to acknowledge and thank my step-mother, Alice Lora, and step-sister, Leah Ray, for their continuous love and kindness, and support throughout my life. A deep thank you to my step-brother, Jeff Ray, who passed in 2014 at the young age of 43, with whom I shared a deep bond and who reminded me to follow my passion by his demonstration of following his own.

My gratitude goes to both Michael J Tamura—a wonderful Author, Spiritual Teacher, and Clairvoyant Visionary—whom I consider a great friend and a living example of joy, who also wrote the foreword for this book, and Gabriela Ilie, a loyal and supportive friend, and loving Spirit.

My sincere thanks to the late, great Dr. Kenneth Wapnick, the beloved teacher and most prolific writer about A Course in Miracles, who really understood the teachings of Jesus. I have received much inspiration in my study and practice of the Course from both him and his lovely wife, Gloria Wapnick, founders of the Foundation for A Course in Miracles.

Last, but not least, a heartfelt thank you to the authorized publisher and copyright holder of A Course in Miracles, *The Foundation for Inner Peace,* for their years of dedication in making the Course available to millions of people around the world.

Cindy Lora-Renard

CHAPTER 1

AN INTRODUCTION TO PURE NON-DUALISM

Knowledge is truth, under one law, the law of love or God.
Truth is unalterable, eternal and unambiguous. It can be
unrecognized, but it cannot be changed. It applies to everything
that God created, and only what He created is real. [1]

On May 6, 2019, the 13th anniversary of when my husband, Gary, and I met for the first time (in this lifetime) I received a beautiful visitation by Jesus in a dream, which was more like a mystical vision. He was sitting on a desk in an office type atmosphere with his legs swinging back and forth playfully, like a child. I was in the room, looking down at what I was doing when I heard the most beautiful, yet authoritative and loving male voice start speaking. I looked up and noticed he was looking directly at me with intensity. He playfully motioned for me to come to where he was sitting. Of course I walked over to him. I telepathically received the message that he wanted me to observe two people, a man and a woman, having a conversation. He wanted me to watch their eyes as they spoke. The man wasn't being authentic, and the woman was annoyed because of it. Another telepathic message came to me from Jesus: "Maybe the man isn't being authentic, but what matters most in a situation like this is that *you* are authentically watching it from an honest place, from your right mind. This can't happen until you remove your own inauthentic blocks, the blocks to the awareness of love's presence. If someone is in their ego and we are watching it

1

with *our* egos, what do we get in return? What is the payoff? More ego. This means we are in need of the Atonement or healing."

Note: *The meaning of Atonement in A Course in Miracles, which is what the material in this book is based on, is not to be confused with the Biblical idea of Atonement; that you have to atone for your sins. A Course in Miracles says there is no sin, so Atonement as explained in the Course means that one accepts the idea that the separation from God has not occurred, and that is why we are all innocent. Atonement is healing the belief in separation from each other and from God, accepting God as the **only** reality, which is pure non-dualism.*

The telepathic message continued: "The person standing before you isn't even there, because it's your projection, so who needs the healing if there is ego or separation involved? You do. The story of the past, present, and future of the world is written. Think of a book. All of the content is already written. You are just re-reading the story you wrote, but forgot you wrote it. In time, it appeared to happen a long time ago and now you are watching it as an observer in the mind. The events in the story are neutral. In fact, every experience you have is neutral until you give it meaning. When you give it your own meaning or interpretation you suffer. There is another voice you can listen to, the Voice of the Holy Spirit, which will help you re-interpret this story or dream that you made up. The closest you can be to yourself as God created you is to see God in everyone and be as honest or authentic as you can in this process. The truly honest are in their right minds. There is no conflict until you interpret a situation with the ego instead of choosing the alternative. When you invest in the ego, you invest in nothing, and your return will be nothing, and you will pay the price for it, experiencing yourself as joyless or *not* as God created you. All of you who walk this world have rehearsed your parts very well in the play of life. Look for meaning in this play-not in the play, but in whose version of it you listen to, the ego or Holy Spirit. You have let people and the world be the leaders that pull you around. Let God be the driver, not people. The ego can sit in the backseat. The body and world, which is also a body, is not the decision-maker. You may use your mind to make decisions, but when truth wholly enters your mind, decisions disappear and only truth remains, and there is nothing left to decide."

I woke up from the dream and realized I had just had a profound experience. I always know when the dream is inspired because I wake up with chills, and a rush of energy moves through me. I thanked Jesus for the way he presented the information to me, deepening my understanding of pure non-dualism, which partly means that one is vigilant *only* for God, the only reality there is. I also took away the idea that when we join with God first in our minds, which means *not* thinking with the ego, then that is the only meaningful decision we can make. Everything else will fall into place.

In light of the story above, I wish to reiterate that this book is being written for the purpose of clarifying what it means to practice pure non-dualism, which is the idea that God is the only reality, and since we (all of us as one) are a part of God, we are one with Him in this reality. How do we incorporate this idea into our everyday lives? In the many workshops I do with my husband, author Gary R. Renard, we receive many questions about the Course, especially in the areas of forgiveness, which leads us to the understanding that we aren't separate from each other. This book will help to clarify what true forgiveness means and how to apply it in your everyday life, which speeds up the process of undoing the ego and experiencing your true nature as invulnerable Spirit. Also, an understanding of pure non-dualism is necessary before one can begin to grasp the true meaning of forgiveness as discussed in the Course. Ultimately, true forgiveness will lead you to awakening from the dream of separation.

As we go along, many of the terms used in the Course will be explained with some examples to help further one's understanding. Whether you are new to the Course, or if you've been a student of it for many years doesn't matter. This book was written both as a reinforcement of the ideas presented in the Course, including some of its most advanced principles for continuing students, and also to serve as an introduction to those who may be a bit more unfamiliar with the teachings. Either way, it can serve anyone who wishes to continue their learning on the path of awakening from the dream of separation.

I recognize, too, that I am not perfect, and I have my own forgiveness lessons just like anyone else. I will be sharing some personal examples of how I continue to work through my own lessons and bring myself back to a place of peace.

The Course is very practical in that it gives us a series of lessons in the Workbook that helps one to bring about the experience of the principles it is teaching us in the text. Application of its principles on a daily basis is a necessary component in helping us achieve the goal the Course sets forth, the attainment of true peace. If you want to learn more about Helen Schucman, the scribe of the Course, and the story of how the Course came into being, I recommend reading *Absence from Felicity* by Dr. Kenneth Wapnick, Ph.D. It is a journey into Helen's process as she was developing her relationship with Jesus, preparing the way for her to scribe the Course.

If you've ever wondered what it would be like to learn from a spiritual master such as Jesus, then you will find his original teachings in the Course, which is what he taught 2000 years ago. He was making a clear distinction between the real and the unreal. As he says in his Course, *Nothing real can be threatened. Nothing unreal exists. Herein lies the peace of God.*[2] This takes some spiritual background to understand. The meaning behind the statement above is that what is real is God or perfect love. What is unreal is anything that opposes this perfect love of God, which means anything that can shift or change or take on a form of some kind. With this understanding, there is peace. These ideas will become clearer to you as we go along, especially the idea that nothing truly exists but God. Practice brings about this understanding. I was amused when I saw a cartoon once where a guru was sitting quietly meditating, and someone approached him and said, "Hey, how's nothing?" Just to clarify, even if you accept non-dualism as pure truth, I don't recommend you approach people, especially if they are hurting, and say "How's nothing?" In other words, it's good to be normal and appropriate with people even if you know the world is an illusion. But it's fun to know the truth!

The *real* you is perfect Spirit, whole and innocent, still at home in God. We are merely dreaming a dream that we are living in a world of time and space, and have become so identified with our stories that we forgot where we came from and who created us. If God is perfect love, then so are you, because He created you in His likeness. There can be nothing outside this love, but there can be a belief that there is something else. The Course helps one to train the mind to think as the Holy Spirit thinks, who only knows love, innocence, wholeness and joy. The Holy Spirit sees our illusions without believing in them. That is why we can trust Him to guide us toward the highest good of all concerned. We just need to ask for help.

The Course is not a religion even though it uses Christian terminology. It does so for a reason as it speaks to a Western audience. Jesus is clearly "correcting" some of the misinterpretations of his teachings from 2000 years ago, only for the purpose of clarifying what he really meant. His message got distorted over time (kind of like the game telephone) and there were certain groups that wanted to suppress the information for purposes of furthering their agenda of control. The idea that God is love and is the *only* reality also got distorted by the story the ego told us at the beginning, which is that we *did* separate from Him. The story of the ego is a lie. It requires the undoing of the ego to fully experience the *true* nature of reality.

I grew up Protestant, frequently going to a mainstream Methodist Church. I liked the social aspect of Church, and had an outstanding and loving minister, but I never really resonated with the kind of Jesus that was being presented to me while growing up. Maybe that is why my sister and I, very young at the time, would find ways to amuse ourselves and make ourselves laugh by passing funny notes back and forth to each other when we were supposed to be quiet during the sermon. One way we would do this is to quote funny lines from movies we liked. So, one Sunday morning during a sermon my sister really got me going and I couldn't hold in my laughter. She passed me a note that said, "I can fart the theme to jaws." Needless to say, I was completely defeated in my ability to be quiet for the rest of the sermon. My point is that sometimes we do things for ourselves to bring about some sort of relief against something else that the mind is resisting. In my case, laughter brings that much needed relief when things get too serious, or if I'm being presented with information that doesn't make sense to me. This still happens today, laughter being my release under intense circumstances.

Later in life (under unique circumstances), I found myself attending the Sunday services conducted by the famous singer and actress, Della Reese. She was such a breath of fresh air! Her animated way of delivering a speech and her powerful singing voice was my cup of tea! I was also a big fan of the hit TV show, "Touched by an Angel." So I thought it was really cool that she was making herself available to the public with a weekly Sunday service. Little did I know that a few years later she would be performing the marriage ceremony of my former husband Steve and me, as well as give me a private, inspired speech about life. Those were interesting days!

I want to be clear that I don't disrespect one's choices as to how or to whom they pray, or to whom one chooses to listen to find the truth. There are many paths that lead to God. I am merely following the path that was meant for me. I fully resonate with what Jesus is saying in A Course in Miracles. For me, it speaks the truth so I have been guided to share my experience with it, and the benefits of learning from one of the greatest masters in the history of our illusory world. I will get more into the illusory nature of the world as we go along.

The Course doesn't claim to be the only path to God, but it is a faster way home because it gets right to the root cause of all suffering, which is guilt over the belief we separated from God. This guilt is unconscious to us, which is why most people don't know that guilt is what's driving all forms of suffering on the planet. The Course tells us how that appeared to happen, and what to do about it *now*. When you remove guilt from the mind, there is no suffering. This is why Jesus didn't suffer on the cross, which he also explains in the section in the Course about the crucifixion. He had forgiven the world, not because it did something to him; rather, he knew it was a projection coming from the one mind (all of us as one) that believed in the separation. He wasn't *in* the dream, but the dreamer of the dream, just like all of us are. This means he wasn't at the effect of a world that wasn't really there. Another way of saying what he may have experienced on the cross was that he entered a state of Samadhi, which is *a state of intense concentration achieved through meditation. In Hindu yoga, this is regarded as the final stage, at which union with the divine is reached (before or at death).*[3] **As you will see, the Course is not saying the same thing as other systems of thought. It is a totally unique thought system and makes total sense when you put all the pieces of the puzzle together, which is a process that occurs over time. When you start to see the whole picture, understanding returns.**

Have you ever asked yourself, will I ever find peace? When will this pain end? Is there an end to suffering? Or even, why is there so much suffering in the world? Why can't people just get along? Why can't I get along with my partner, friend, sibling, parent or co-worker? Why can't they get along with me? What is fueling this anger, resentment, sadness or judgment? All of these common questions (which most of us have asked from time to time) have an answer. The answer may not be what you expect, but I can assure you that when you accept the answer, you will experience the kind of peace we all seek - the ability to be peaceful regardless of circumstances. It's also important to maintain a sense of humor, which is a quality of an enlightened being. We can take ourselves so seriously and forget to laugh. The process of undoing the ego so that we can experience the attainment of true peace can be intense, because it asks us to question every value we hold. It's not easy letting go of self-concepts that we think are very important and real. This is precisely why humor is necessary.

I've always enjoyed the comedy of the comedian, Bob Newhart. He has a brilliant way of stating things with a totally straight face, which makes what he is saying even funnier. I have a story about meeting Bob Newhart and Don Rickles. The parents of my former husband, Steve, knew both Bob and Don, and we were all invited to a party at Don Rickles' house. The first thing Don Rickles said to Steve when we walked in was, "Steve, why is it every time I see you I get pissed off!" That was pretty funny. Later that evening, I found myself standing between Bob Newhart and Don Rickles, and I actually had the nerve to start telling them a joke! I told my joke and they laughed. I breathed a sigh of relief. I'll be talking more about the importance of humor in a later chapter.

The problem most of us have is that we look for the answer to life's problems where it is not found, outside of ourselves. In fact, the Course explains to us that when we are perceiving a world at all, we are caught in a dream. In reality or God, there is nothing to perceive. Heaven/God is the awareness of perfect oneness. So there is really nothing outside of us, which means the world is a projection coming from a split mind that believes in separation. This includes every form of life in the world and universe we've made real: humans, animals, plants, insects, other planets, E.T.'s, and the list goes on and on. This may be shocking to some, but *all your time is spent in dreaming. Your sleeping and your waking dreams have different forms, and that is all. Their content is the same. They are your protest against reality, and your fixed and insane idea that you can change it.*[4]

The mind that appears to be split can be thought of as tri-partite in nature: The wrong mind, the right mind, and the decision-maker that chooses between the two. The Course also uses the word ego to mean the wrong part of the mind, which is the part of our minds that believes we are separate from each other and God, and then we act that out. The right mind can be referred to as the Holy Spirit, or our memory of God, or the Voice that speaks for God. Jesus can be thought of as the Holy Spirit, since he has awakened from the dream of separation, so I will be using his name and the Holy Spirit interchangeably. The right part of the mind, when we choose it, leads us to peace, whereas the ego leads us to pain. The decision-maker is what chooses between the two at any given moment.

Whichever one you choose will make the experience you have, because each one gives you a different version of the story. The ego always sees attack, which makes anger justified. The Holy Spirit sees only calls for love and expressions of love, an idea I will be repeating often. If someone is calling out for love, which one can do in many different and vicious ways, the response should be love. And, of course, if one is expressing love, the response is the same: love.

We all need encouragement to reinforce the idea that we always have a choice as to how we interpret what our body's eyes are showing us. These ideas train the mind to help you remember that you are pure love because that is how you were created. If you are trying to be something different, you are introducing conflict into your life unnecessarily. The practical part of this, or how to apply it in your everyday life, will be explained as we go along. This of course doesn't mean that you become a doormat and let people walk all over you. It doesn't mean you don't take care of yourself. You can do these "normal" things, but with the Holy Spirit as your teacher instead of the ego. Your life will become happier and more peaceful as you practice.

So, if the world (which feels very real) is a dream, and God is the only reality, how did we appear to get here? As the Course asks us, *Who is the "you" who are living in this world? Spirit is immortal, and immortality is a constant state. It is as true now as it ever was or ever will be, because it implies no change at all. It is not a continuum, nor is it understood by being compared to an opposite. Knowledge never involves comparisons.*[5] This answers the question for those who may be unsure as to whether or not God created the world. In other words, God would not need to experience Himself by creating a world of duality (a popular New Age idea) and a world of suffering. That would make God, who is perfect love, an insane God. To repeat, pure non-dualism means there is *only* God, and nothing else. If God is absolute reality, there can be nothing else to oppose that idea. It is the observer or decision-making part of your mind that is mentally reviewing yourself and the world from another level. You are Spirit, not a body. You are only having an experience that you are in a body and in a world of time and space. The *experience* we are having here certainly *seems* real, but it's not true.

Coming back to how we appeared to get here, the Course says that *Into eternity, where all is one, there crept a tiny, mad idea, at which the Son of God remembered not to laugh. In his forgetting did the thought become a serious idea, and possible of both accomplishment and real effects. Together, we can laugh them both away, and understand that time cannot intrude upon eternity. It is a joke to think that time can come to circumvent eternity, which means there is no time.*[6] This statement is telling us that the cause of all of the ideas and concepts we made up that seem to make time real, such as attacking each other, seeing others as our enemies, and thinking our minds are in our bodies, are really the result of the belief we separated from God, feel guilty over that, and now secretly believe we deserve to be punished for it. We projected onto God the belief He is now a vengeful God coming back to punish us for our "sin" of what we think we really did to Him. This may be the origin of the unfortunate phrase, "God fearing person," but usually it means "I believe in God." It's important to remember that God need not be feared, because God doesn't know about fear. He didn't make it. He is perfect love and so are you. So the world we now see is a projection of the terrible thing we thought we did to God, leaving Him, and substituting a "better" world to replace the Kingdom of Heaven. This doesn't mean we are really guilty. Just as children wander off on their own, thinking they know best, and then get lost, we are like those children. We wandered off innocently from our true home, thinking we knew better, and then started paying the price for that by feeling separate, lonely and afraid for the first time.

I'd like to recommend a few movies, with themes of forgiveness, that Gary and I found very inspiring. Since we love movies, we enjoy sharing some of our favorites with people. Instead of going into detail about the films, I'll just list them and allow you to enjoy the deeper meaning of them if you decide to watch them:

1. The Shack
2. As it is in Heaven
3. Simon Burch

Although these are dramas, it's also good to watch funny movies when you can since things can feel heavy at times. Seriousness can take a toll on our health and well-being, so laughter can help bring about balance, reminding us of the lightness that is our true nature.

Shifting our perceptions to reflect the truth brings about fear, because we fear change. The reason lots of us fear change is because it reminds us of the first change we ever experienced: being separate from our Creator. God just wants us to come home. He can't see our dreams of pain and hatred, and wouldn't acknowledge them if he could, because that would make the dream real. He just knows his children are asleep, having a nightmare, and wants them to return to the home they've never truly left. *It's just a dream.* A dream of separation is not real separation. I will get to how one can undo the ego and wake up from this dream in the next chapter, which focuses on true forgiveness, the process which undoes the guilt in the unconscious mind over the separation. Even though the world itself is an illusion, it doesn't mean we should ignore it. Afterall, this is our experience, and we all have our scripts where we are learning our lessons of forgiveness. We are drawn to certain people, careers, hobbies, etc. There is a reason for that, so it's appropriate to follow our intuition the best we can and be guided along our path to awakening.

I remember when I first read about the idea that God did not create the world. It didn't seem unusual to me; it made a lot of sense. How many of us have asked the question, "How could a God make a world like this, with so much suffering and pain?" For me, personally, it made total sense that if God is perfect love, then He can't be anything else. He wouldn't need to create something opposite to that to prove He exists. It seems so silly. That was how I thought of it. It didn't feel like a big deal to me. It was actually a relief! This gives us a perfect, loving God to return home to. This is very comforting.

The world has also been confused about the mind/brain problem. The mind isn't in the body. The body is in the mind, just as the whole world is in the mind of the dreamer. This also includes the brain. The brain doesn't think, just as eyes don't see, and ears don't hear. It's the mind that does these things, using the body as a vehicle. The organs of our bodies only do what the mind directs. When you are dreaming in bed at night, you are seeing all kinds of images. You aren't seeing those images with the body's eyes, because they are closed. You are seeing them with your mind. The same thing applies to feelings or effects of our dreams. It is the mind that feels them. There is a tendency to confuse levels when it comes to the Course. It is written on two levels, the metaphysical level of reality, and the level of the world of form, which is our experience. So, as you read the statements above about how the brain, eyes, and ears don't really do anything, it doesn't mean you don't take care of yourself at the body level. It just means that when it comes to how you *think* about yourself and the world, there is a perspective of reality that you can hold which keeps you at the cause of your experience, so that you don't have to live your life being at the effect of the world. This keeps you in control of *how* you experience yourself and the world.

If we are dreaming a dream, we can change our minds *about* the dream. That is the one true power we have in this world. When you shift from being at the effect of your dream to the cause of it, you are placing yourself in a position of true power, so you don't have to be a victim of the images you are seeing. Practice not letting anyone, whether it's your own government, special people in your life, or anyone in general be the source of your upset. It weakens you as a Son of God. And the Son of God (all of us as one) wasn't created in weakness. Weakness only comes from the belief we are something different than our Creator. The world isn't the decision-maker and doesn't decide for you. *You* are the decision-maker because you are a mind and not a body. This is how you can live in a world of time and space and not be a victim of the world you see. It doesn't mean you shouldn't have compassion and empathy for those that may be suffering, only that you don't have to join in their dream of pain, which is sympathy. Empathy is having the capacity to understand the pain others go through, but without becoming personally attached to it. That is a pretty big difference. You can do this by staying in your right mind the best you can as you interact with people and remember the truth of your oneness with God. This also means that it is wise to still follow the "basic" laws that we are given in the world, because that is common sense, but it doesn't mean you have to let the laws we have here dictate how you feel. You can still know and trust in your mind that at a "higher" level, we truly operate under God's law, or the Law of Love.

The goal of the Course is the attainment of true peace. True peace means that you are peaceful regardless of circumstances. From the perspective of the Course, if the world is a dream, then why would one thing in a dream appear to be harder to overcome than another part of the dream, unless you are making it real? In other words, there isn't really a hierarchy of problems in a dream, because they are all untrue, and stem from the only problem or lack that we need to correct, which is a sense of separation from God. Of course it takes practice to really think this way. Lots of practice! All of the contents in a dream fall under one category: they are all equally untrue. It's all part of a movie that's already been filmed.

I'll never forget the time Gary and I went to see a movie, and I had an experience that deepened my understanding that the world is nothing but a projection coming from the mind. I had been asking the Holy Spirit for help with healing my anxiety that was triggered by being in the middle of a large crowd of people, with no easy exit. This started during a lifetime I had as a disciple of Jesus. There were some intense times during those days, and it was explained to me by Spirit that I witnessed people threatening Jesus's life. Also, he occasionally had very large crowds around him. For me, it felt suffocating and frightening. I apparently carried some of that over in this lifetime, and I still tend to feel that intensity when I feel suffocated or in the middle of a crowd. What triggered my first experience of anxiety in the form of a panic attack in this lifetime was when I was touring a museum. I looked at a painting of Jesus who was preaching to a group of people who were surrounding him. This apparently triggered a memory of some of the more intense times the disciples went through during that time. Of course, the root cause of all anxiety, depression, or whatever it is one may be experiencing can always be traced back to the belief we are guilty over having separated from God. That is what needs to be forgiven over time. One should allow that process to unfold without judging the self. Dealing with intense feelings of anxiety or depression can feel devastatingly "real," so it's a normal thing to do whatever you can to take care of yourself and seek help in whatever form is most helpful and loving. I will address depression, anxiety, and suicide in Chapter 4.

Back to my movie experience with Gary: We were in the theater. The movie started playing. I suddenly looked up toward the projector, which I rarely ever do. I saw the light from the projector with all the particles floating in the light from the projector, and then followed the beam of light to the screen where all the images were appearing. Although I knew the mind projects the body and the world, just as the projector in a movie theater projects the images on the screen, I experienced this fact at a deeper level. For example, I was reminded that the 50 people or so that were projected onto the movie screen only had one projector projecting all of them. You don't need 50 projectors for 50 people to appear on the screen. One projector projects it all. Similarly, the larger mind works the same way. There is only one mind projecting the 7 billion or so people on the planet. There aren't 7 billion minds projecting although it looks and seems that way. There is only one mind, the ego part of the split mind that is projecting the whole world and all the people in the world we see. All of us appear to have a unique point of view because each of us believes we are separate. This is the ultimate illusion. When the mind is whole, there are no points of view because there are no choices to choose between. There is no world of perception. There is only God, or awareness of perfect oneness. In fact, the Course says, *There is no world! This is the central thought the course attempts to teach. Not everyone is ready to accept it, and each one must go as far as he can let himself be led along the road to truth. He will return and go still farther, or perhaps step back a while and then return again.*[7] In other words, we are all on the path home to God, but until we fully accept the Atonement for ourselves for the final time, we will appear to come back (reincarnate) until all our lessons are learned.

I got a kick out of another non-dualist type cartoon I saw with an image of someone saying, "As an avid believer in absolutely nothing, I am deeply pained when literally anything occurs."

The Illusion of Time

In order to truly understand pure non-dualism, it is also helpful to have a grasp of the illusory nature of time and space, and what projecting a world of time and space entails. I've always been fascinated by the topic of time, and how the Course speaks about it. The dream script of time includes every possibility that has been thought, and time all happened in one instant. If there is a "big bang," then that was the big bang, the idea that all of time (past, present, and future) occurred at the same time - the instant the thought of separation got projected outward. This means evolution is not what it seems, since everything already happened, and time is holographic, not linear. Thus, evolution can be thought of as a correction of the Divine presence. In other words, as we are working on bringing the ego's thought system of sin, guilt, and fear to the correction of the Holy Spirit (our innocence) we are undoing separation and moving closer to enlightenment. **This is the purpose of time: correcting our misperceptions, and then time collapses. Eventually, time and the universe will disappear, when the mind that made time lets go of the belief in it.**

Time is really a defense against the truth of our oneness. It was made by the ego mind to escape reality, believing that if we returned to reality, we would surely be punished by God over the separation (as explained above). Remember, the ego made up a God in its own image, which has nothing to do with love. The Course explains to us that in that same instant the thought of separation, which gave rise to time, occurred, God gave the correction for time. The Course puts it this way: *Time lasted but an instant in your mind, with no effect upon eternity. And so is all time past, and everything exactly as it was before the way to nothingness was made. The tiny tick of time in which the first mistake was made, and all of them within that one mistake, held also the Correction for that one, and all of them that came within the first. And in that tiny instant time was gone, for that was all it ever was.*[8] In other words, time is over, but we are re-living it as if it were happening now. Another quote from the Course that may be helpful about time is this: *Time seems to go in one direction, but when you reach its end it will roll up like a long carpet spread along the past behind you, and will disappear. As long as you believe the Son of God is guilty you will walk along this carpet, believing that it leads to death. And the journey will seem long and cruel and senseless, for so it is.*[9]

So, what keeps us on the carpet of time is guilt. Until we forgive the world for what it has *not* done to us (the true meaning of forgiveness) we will continue to walk the carpet of time. The purpose of time is to heal through forgiveness of ourselves and others, and wake up from the dream of separation. The journey will only seem cruel, and long and hard, when we hold on to grievances and judgments. When we let them go, and forgive the guilt associated with them, we will experience the joy in which we were created. I like to say, "The world is the great projection. The Holy Spirit is the great correction." I will get into methods of application and exercises in later chapters.

Top Five Differences between the New Age and A Course in Miracles

One day I was sitting around thinking about the uniqueness of the Course, and how its pure non-dualistic thought system isn't saying the same thing as anything else. The Course not only describes the one and only problem we have, but also gives the answer to the problem. It gives us a Workbook of 365 lessons to train the mind to undo the ego, and awaken to our true nature as love. Through practice and patience, salvation will be ours. Salvation is to be free of the ego's perception. This means we give up our attack thoughts and replace them with the thoughts of the Holy Spirit. Also, the Course doesn't hold back when it comes to explaining the ego's strategy in making up the world. It's not a pretty picture, although we can use what the ego made and shift its purpose to reflect forgiveness, which transforms the meaning of the images we see into something that can reflect the love of the Holy Spirit. As I was thinking about this, I started to write out some of the key differences between the Course and the New Age movement. The statements below are to be taken within the context of pure non-dualism, and that nothing God didn't create can be in our best interests. It may help you to question every value you hold and consider what is truly important as you navigate this dream we call life.

Some of the statements below are a direct quote from the Course, and I've paraphrased some of the others to reflect some of the general ideas in the Course:

1. **The New Age says: Birth is a miracle. The Course says: Children are born into it through pain and in pain. Their growth**

is attended by suffering, and they learn of sorrow and separation and death.[10]

2. The New Age says: God created the world and saw that it was good. The Course says: God doesn't even know about the world, because He didn't create it.

3. The New Age says: The body is beautiful and holy. The Course says: Can you paint rosy lips on a skeleton, pet it and pamper it, and make it live?[11]

4. The New Age says: The world is a holy place. The Course says: The world you see is the delusional system of those made mad by guilt.[12]

5. The New Age says: Think positive thoughts, and make the ego your friend. The Course says: Your thoughts are not real and the ego wants to kill you.

I'd like to put all this into context so it doesn't seem as if the Course is negative, which it is not. Remember, the Course is saying that God is the only reality and nothing can oppose this reality. God doesn't take form, and there is no shift or change in God or Heaven. However, when we are caught in a world of time and space (which is the world of perception), we are caught in a false dream of duality that *seems* real. There is a subject and an object. This world was made by fear, not by love, because it's a projection of the thought of separation that we made real in the mind before that thought got projected outward, and made a world of time and space. **There is nothing beautiful about the ego. *Thinking* with the ego is what brings us pain. The best thing we can do is undo it.**

The good news is that you can shift the purpose of what the made-up world is for, using it for the Holy Spirit's purpose of forgiveness, which awakens you from the dream of separation, and leads you back to your true home in God/Heaven, which you've never really left. This is what makes us truly happy. The thoughts we think with the ego aren't real, and that's what the statement above means. Only thoughts that are inspired by love are our real thoughts. In Heaven, we don't even need to think, because we are being thought by God.

Also, the ideas above can be better understood when you recognize that this world is not a happy place in and of itself. We are born, and then we die, over and over again. There is sickness and separation everywhere, murder, judgments, blame, and the list goes on. Can this be the happy world? Once you see it for what it is, the best thing we can do is wake up from what we think is our life here, to our true life with God. **True happiness comes when we realize we are not even here. We've gone to sleep in Heaven, and we are dreaming we are in hell**. To clarify, Heaven is joining, and hell is separation. I've always been a very positive person by nature, but I can surely see that this world was not made by love. Love can be reflected here, but the love we seek in relationships is not the same as the pure love of God. I'll get to that when I discuss special relationships in Chapter 6.

The reference above to children being born in pain is just referring to the idea that pain is not of God, nor is birth something that really happens to any of us. Both birth and death are illusions of a mind that is dreaming. This doesn't mean you shouldn't have children if you are guided to. Your decision to have children can be guided by the Holy Spirit. All our relationships here, whether they are with children or anyone else, are meant to be used as classrooms to learn our lessons of forgiveness. We are learning to transform all our "special relationships" into holy ones, so they can serve a holy purpose.

To repeat, the Course is one path among many that leads to God, so it is not saying it's the only path. It does say it can save you time. This is because it gets to the root cause of all suffering, which, again, is guilt over the belief we have separated from God. We tried to pull this off, but it didn't work, thank goodness! The Course will lead you to a happy dream, so that instead of seeing a vicious world full of anger, hatred, and murder, you can learn to see it as a classroom where you learn your lessons of forgiveness. When the world is used for this purpose, it changes the experience you have while you appear to be here. The images you see can be transformed into loveliness when their purpose has been shifted to reflect the thought system of the Holy Spirit.

To review, this is what it means to accept the Atonement for one-self: Atonement is the recognition that the separation from God hasn't occurred. So, the Course encourages us by saying that we each need to accept that for ourselves, which is a process that happens over time. There is no need to rush this process, but let it unfold with Grace. Also, since there is only one mind, and you think of yourself as part of this one mind, then it would have to follow that there is only one dreamer or projector of the dream, and you're it, because there is no one else out there. There is an illusion of billions of different people, but it all comes from one source or one mind that is projecting. So, from my perspective, I would acknowledge that I (meaning the one decision-making mind) am dreaming the dream and I can take responsibility for how I interpret the dream. It is not me, Cindy the personality, dreaming the dream, but the larger ego mind that is dreaming. This persona, Cindy, is just part of the projection. It is not my identity. This doesn't mean we are responsible for other people's behavior. Everyone who believes they are here will eventually accept the Atonement for himself/herself. This is how the mind becomes whole again in our experience. **The mind will stop reviewing the script of time and space when every last part of the mind accepts the Atonement. Then, the universe will disappear, because the only thing holding it together is our belief in it**.

Life can be fun when you understand how the nature of the mind works! Gary and I often say that we enjoy life more knowing it's an illusion, even though we still have our forgiveness lessons. We are still normal in the dream, and follow our natural guidance or intuition, which can lead to a synchronistic flow of life events. At some point along the journey, a natural process occurs within oneself that inspires the following questions, "How will all this end? Is it logical to think that we keep experiencing reincarnation forever?" The answers to these questions are inherent in the explanation of pure non-dualism above. In other words, *The world will end in an illusion, as it began. Yet will its ending be an illusion of mercy.*[13] Inherent in the above statement is the realization that we never truly incarnated. So, my hope is that in reading these pages you see it as an adventure into a whole new way of thinking about yourself, others, the world and life in general. Here we go!

Page for Personal Notes

CHAPTER 2

TRUE FORGIVENESS VS. FORGIVENESS TO DESTROY

Forgiveness, truly given, is the way in which your only hope of freedom lies. Others will make mistakes and so will you, as long as this illusion of a world appears to be your home.[1]

Back in the early 2000's when I was still married to my former husband, Steve, we went on a trip to the beautiful country of Greece, where Steve's sister lived, in Athens. We explored some breathtaking places, including the Parthenon, as well as a trip to Delphi. I do recommend that people go visit this most ancient and beautiful country. I've always respected how some cultures retain the beauty of some of the oldest structures on earth. It keeps life interesting and adventurous! While we were visiting there, little did I know that an experience I had witnessed with Steve's sister's husband would provide me with a forgiveness lesson, which over time I learned to forgive. Everyone has things that take form for them in certain ways that provide incredible forgiveness opportunities. For me, one of those forms is when I see animal abuse, although through the practice of forgiveness over many years, I have become more peaceful in general about everything. I have always been sensitive to animals, and regard them as highly spiritual beings that provide us with unconditional love and acceptance. They are easy to love.

So, one of the days we were there, Steve's sister and her husband, whom I'll call Andreas for the sake of privacy, had a party at their house where we were staying. It was a lively party with about 25 people in attendance. Andreas, from what I had seen up to that point, had a drinking problem, and was growing more and more intoxicated as the night went on. I wasn't judging him as a person, but it was obvious he had a drinking problem. I was mingling with some guests when I heard a scream coming from the living room. Steve's young niece, about 13 years old at the time, was terrified because one of their dogs was attacking their other dog, who was blind, very small, and incapable of defending himself. Of course, in a situation like this, people would step in to do what they could to keep the dogs apart, and do their best to separate the dogs. They were both small dogs, so it would be fairly easy to just pick up one of them and take them out of the room. Well, Andreas, who was very drunk at this point, ran over to the dog who was attacking the other dog and kicked him as hard as he could. He kicked him so hard and with such viciousness, that the dog flew across the entire living room, landing with a loud bang. The dog was totally in shock and shaking uncontrollably. The other dog ended up being fine, thank goodness, but as soon as I could, I ran over to the dog who had just been kicked out of its mind, and I picked him up and ran upstairs. I could hear Andreas and some of his friends who were also very drunk saying to each other, "Look! She actually cares about the dog! Look what she is doing! She is treating the dog like he is as important as a person!" And then they continued laughing. As I was holding the dog in my arms, tears were streaming down my face, and I was doing my best to console the dog who was still shaking. I was talking to him in a gentle, loving voice being as loving as I could. I continued to remain upstairs consoling the dog until he calmed down a bit. Fortunately, he also seemed okay physically, but was obviously emotionally traumatized. Later that evening, almost everyone in Andreas' family was defending his behavior, except for Steve, who understood that what we witnessed was abuse that could have killed one or even both dogs.

I bring up this story because at the time, I wasn't practicing the Course, so I hadn't learned about the kind of forgiveness the Course was teaching. This provided me with a tremendous forgiveness opportunity, which I did forgive. Once I learned what true forgiveness meant, I was actually relieved! It was helpful to know that I didn't have to be a victim of circumstances, and that I could practice changing my mind about what I was seeing. Most people have a couple bigger forgiveness lessons in their lifetime to work through along with some seeming smaller ones, but the forgiveness process is the same, regardless of how big or small something appears to be. In my process with the example above, looking back post-Course, I remembered that Andreas was really Spirit, whole and innocent, and he didn't have to be the cause of my upset. I could change my mind about him and the situation. This doesn't mean that if I see abuse again, that I wouldn't do something about it. You can be guided by the Holy Spirit to take action that is for the highest good of all concerned.

In light of my personal example above, I would like to expand further on how one can think about abuse, whatever form it takes. Along with practicing true forgiveness, which will soon be explained, look at the abuse or uncomfortable memory you are holding from the past and work with the idea that there is no sin in yourself or the perpetrators, then forgive the guilt associated with that now, in the present, and then you are automatically released from the fear of the belief in punishment on the self from God over the shame you might feel. Remember, we projected onto God a punishing intent, and believed He is enraged over the separation, and will come back to punish us. This is insane. God is perfect love. His Will is one with yours. This means that you and everyone else are worthy of His love. Once you have had time to process the abuse, looking at the pain with the Holy Spirit, you can move into forgiveness. This may take some time, but it can be done. It is done already, but we aren't experiencing our lives from that perspective. Allow yourself the kindness and patience it may take to heal.

I want to share with you, now, the true meaning of forgiveness, how to apply it in your everyday life, and also how to be "normal" in a world where you appear to exist, even when chaos seems to swirl around you. It is also necessary to understand the ego's tricks it plays in making us feel we have really forgiven something when we haven't. So, I will clarify both true forgiveness, and what the Course calls "forgiveness to destroy," which is just a projection, and a misunderstanding of what forgiveness truly means.

Some people who practice the Course might say, "What does it matter what I do if the world is just an illusion?" Regarding the body and our experience here, the Course tells us ...*it is almost impossible to deny its existence in this world. Those who do so are engaging in a particularly unworthy form of denial. The term "unworthy" here implies only that it is not necessary to protect the mind by denying the unmindful. If one denies this unfortunate aspect of the mind's power, one is also denying the power itself.*[2] In other words, it would be wise to respect the power of the mind to choose wrongly, because that same power can choose right-mindedness as well, leading you out of the dream of separation. Also, you can still learn your lessons of forgiveness and be peaceful even in the midst of turmoil. Just shrugging off the world because it doesn't exist is just another ego trick to keep one rooted further in the dream of separation. As long as we believe we are bodies living in a world of time and space, it wouldn't do us much good to pretend it doesn't exist. We still need to take care of ourselves, and exercise compassion for ourselves and others. The ego still needs to be undone. Making a decision to undo the ego through forgiveness requires a realization that the world isn't what truly makes us happy. The world, if you look closely, is not a happy place. This doesn't mean that you can't be happy here; you can. It only means that you will no longer desire anything in the world to bring about your happiness. Only God's love will ever fulfill you, because God is fulfillment itself; it is a state of joy.

True Forgiveness

Forgiveness, if properly understood, is recognizing that what you thought another has done to you has not really occurred. A little more explaining is required here. This kind of forgiveness is understood only at the level of truth, or absolute reality. When it is recognized that God's love doesn't disappear despite the vicious behavior of others, you can remember that God's love can be chosen regardless of circumstances instead of the ego's need to reinforce guilt and fear in yourself and others. This is because the separation from God is an illusion, which means we've never left God. This is why we are all innocent, seeming victims and perpetrators alike. In this context, true forgiveness means we overlook the errors of others, which means we don't make the error real at the mind level. To forgive *is* to heal.

I would like to offer an example: Let's say someone says something very unkind to you during a conversation. You were at peace before they said it to you, and now your peace is gone because of what this person said. With true forgiveness, you would notice what the person said, but you wouldn't make it real in your mind and give that person power to take away the peace of God within you. If you react as though they changed your mind for you, then you just gave your power away to that person. In truth, people don't have that kind of power to change our minds unless we give them that power. Furthermore, they are not really there, because they are part of your dream. If you react to their error of projection, you are making the same mistake they are; making the error real. So, if you are in your right mind and someone says something unkind to you, you wouldn't react with upset. You would understand that they are calling for love, or projecting. In that realization you are free. You would retain your peace knowing it has nothing to do with you. This is why we forgive people for what they haven't done. They haven't truly done anything if you see it with your right mind, and don't take their projections seriously. If we do take it seriously, it only means there is a belief we are holding about ourselves that was already there, and the other person acted as a trigger to bring it out.

In the world, there are certainly consequences for behavior, and it would be wise to follow basic laws while you appear to live in this world. However, you can still overlook and forgive behavior while being normal and doing whatever you are guided to do at this level, with your goal being that whatever happens be for the highest good of all concerned. I like to think of it as my real job is always forgiveness, and then I can practice letting the Holy Spirit guide me to take care of the details the best that I can, but not alone.

Having an attitude of forgiveness means that you are taking full responsibility for your interpretation of what you are seeing. Each one of us is responsible for how we feel. If this weren't the case, then we would indeed be victims of the world we see. There is no power in that, and only makes the world and its problems more real in the mind of the dreamer. So, the overall attitude of one who practices forgiveness recognizes that this is a dream that we are dreaming. We forgive our projected images and ourselves for dreaming them. Then, we turn over the situation to the Holy Spirit, trusting in His strength and wisdom to extend through us, but also that He will do His part, taking care of the bigger picture we can't see.

The mistake that is often made with forgiveness comes from the fact that we've been poorly trained by the ego into believing we are victims. This mindset accuses another for taking one's peace of God away. In other words, we say, "You did this to me, and I was peaceful before you said this to me, and now look at me! I am miserable because of what you did!" We cannot truly forgive someone from this mindset because the cause of our suffering is placed outside of us. This is what it means to give power to the outside. True forgiveness sees past all of this and recognizes that no one can take the peace of God away from you because you are a decision-making mind. Only when you identify with the body can you really be upset, and even destroy the body. The Course says, *Are thoughts, then, dangerous? To bodies, yes!*[3] When you remember that you are not really a body, you can then exercise the power of your mind to choose how you interpret a seeming attack. Remember, all attack is a call for love. This idea will save you.

You get to choose how you interpret something and how you feel about things. No one can choose for you. If someone is calling out for love, which can be expressed in very vicious ways, we need to hear that call, which is in all of us to some degree. Remember we all share the part of the mind that is the ego, as well as the part of the mind that is the Holy Spirit, as well as the decision-maker that chooses between the two. This is why we are the same. People may look different from us, have different religions, sexual preferences, and even our mistakes may take different forms, but we are all the same as equal Sons of God. So, in essence, forgiveness looks past all these differences and sees the call for love behind the facades, and ultimately the innocence in everyone.

In form, we may have to make decisions and report abuse, doing whatever we would normally do to take care of ourselves and respond to others with kindness. But we can forgive and be free in our minds. The reason the Course tells us not to make the errors of others real is because the error of thought that made the world is also an illusion. Choose to love and forgive instead by choosing to see the face of Christ in all your brothers. *Can you remember Him (God) and hate what He created?*[4] In other words, as you see another, you see yourself. Since minds are joined, whatever you are thinking about another person comes right back to you, because it's your projection. If you want to connect with your true nature as Spirit, see only love and innocence in others. You will then come to know yourself. This isn't always easy, and takes lots of practice. No matter how difficult a situation may be, you can still choose to be vigilant in your practice and remember the truth of our oneness. When you understand this kind of forgiveness, you will also understand that all forgiveness is self-forgiveness. This is because we are forgiving in others our own projections, our own belief in sin and hatred. We see our guilt outside of us in other people, which is just how the ego likes it. This is why forgiveness of others is ultimately an illusion, too, because it's our own "stuff" we are seeing in other people that we don't like about ourselves. The Course says we want to see them there and not in ourselves. Yet forgiveness, properly practiced, is what it means to have a happy dream. This is because forgiveness leads to peace, and further awakens us from the dream of separation.

There is still more to understand about forgiveness before we go further, and it is this: *This is the great deception of the world, and you the great deceiver of yourself. It always seems to be another who is evil, and in his sin you are the injured one. How could freedom be possible if this were so? You would be slave to everyone, for what he does entails your fate, your feelings, your despair or hope, your misery or joy.*[5] This is saying that we have lost our freedom as long as we are dependent on someone else to behave a certain way or to be responsible for our misery and pain. When we identify people as evil, we place them beyond forgiveness, in which there is no hope. With true forgiveness, we can free the other and therefore free ourselves. You don't have to agree with them, but you can forgive them. Eventually, you will reach a state where your identification with the ego has been undone, and this self that you think you are will no longer drive your thoughts and actions.

Einstein said, "The true value of a human being is determined primarily by the measure and sense in which he has attained to liberation from the self." Letting go of this self doesn't happen all at once. It is a gradual undoing process. There is no need to be fearful of losing this self. **Sometimes you have to lose yourself to find yourself.** It will happen naturally the more the ego is undone, which happens in stages. We all go through the same stages at different times. We are all on the same path home to God, although it takes different forms. We are the same because we share the same mind.

Here is the meaning of forgiveness in a nutshell: *Forgiveness is the only thing that stands for truth in the illusions of the world. It sees their nothingness, and looks straight through the thousand forms in which they may appear. It looks on lies, but it is not deceived. It does not heed the self-accusing shrieks of sinners mad with guilt. It looks on them with quiet eyes, and merely says to them, "My brother, what you think is not the truth.*[6]

The problem most people have with forgiveness is that there is still a belief that what they are forgiving is the truth instead of illusions. Once it is recognized that the self-concepts we made up are wholly unreal, we can truly forgive anyone or anything. In pure-non-dualism, *only love is real.*

The Steps of Forgiveness

1. *Identify the cause*
2. *Then let it (the cause) go*
3. *So it can be replaced*[7]

In step one, remember that you are never upset for the reason you think. The cause of your upset is having chosen the ego as your teacher. The ego is the teacher of upset. When we think with the ego, we reinforce the separation from each other and from God. This is very painful. We get upset when we allow a person or situation to have power over how we feel because it reminds us that we gave up the power of God when we appeared to separate from His love. This all seemed to occur in the past. We are upset because we are seeing only the past, which is associated with "sin" or separation. We aren't truly seeing anything as it is *now*, or before the illusion of time began. So, we only see what we want to see; we see what we made, not what we are in truth. When we let go of our judgments of people and the world itself, true Vision can be given us, which is the Holy Instant, defined as the instant we choose the Holy Spirit's interpretation instead of the ego's.

One of my favorite quotes in the whole Course that can really help with forgiveness and the letting go of our judgments, grievances, and assumptions about the world we see is the following:

> *Simply do this:*
> *Be still, and lay aside all thoughts of what you are and what God is; all concepts you have learned about the world; all images you hold about yourself. Empty your mind of everything it thinks is either true or false, or good or bad, of every thought it judges worthy, and all the ideas of which it is ashamed. Hold onto nothing. Do not bring with you one thought the past has taught, nor one belief you ever learned before from anything. Forget this world, forget this course, and come with wholly empty hands unto your God.*[8]

In other words, God knows the way to you, so you do not need to know how to get to Him. Our part is to remove the blocks to the awareness of God's love. You can trust that God will do His part. Watch the ego for any demands you place on *how* this should happen. Let it go. *The way to reach Him is merely to let Him be.*[9]

Once we identify the cause of our upset (step 1), we can let the cause go (step 2), which means we are letting go of our interpretation of the problem and the way we set it up. This leaves room for the Holy Spirit to come in (step 3) and help us recognize that our problem has been solved because the separation has been solved. The Holy Spirit is always with us in our minds, but we block it off by insisting that our interpretations are right. We need to let go of the assumption that we understand and know what the problem is so that the answer can be given us. The Holy Spirit will teach us that the only problem we appear to have is the sense of separation from God, which is the only lack we need correct. Acceptance of this comes with practice and patience.

We don't need to do anything about the 3ʳᵈ step, because, after inviting in the Holy Spirit, we will see that what we thought was the problem has already been replaced by the answer, which is that the separation from God has not occurred. This means the world we thought was real has not occurred. Accepting the Atonement for one-self is the answer, and Atonement and healing are identical. Let's review the meaning of Atonement: This is the recognition that the separation from God has not occurred. Nothing has happened. That is why both you and other people are innocent. A dream of separation is not real separation.

It is very important to understand that with this kind of forgiveness it doesn't mean you have to allow people to abuse you in some way. This kind of forgiveness is meant to be practiced at the mind level. It won't make sense if you believe you are a body trapped in time and space. Rather, it requires moving yourself above the battleground of the world to the mind where your real power to choose can be exercised. So you can choose peace in your mind regardless of circumstances, yet still take action if necessary to stop someone from hurting yourself or others. **Forgiveness is medicine for the mind.** When you forgive, the love of your forgiveness will take form in whatever is most helpful for the highest good of all concerned. You can trust that as you make it your goal. You will now be in the business of forgiveness!

Forgiveness-to-Destroy

Before I get into forgiveness-to-destroy, it's time for a little humor: A man was sitting in his chair, calmly meditating, when his wife came into the room and said, "Why can't you meditate on life while you're taking out the garbage?"

Now that we have covered true forgiveness, we can explore for-giveness-to-destroy, which has many forms, but the goal of separation is the same. Forgiveness-to-destroy is the ego's version of forgiveness.

As you will see, it is quite different from true forgiveness as explained above. Although people are well-intentioned, this kind of forgiveness has an unconscious motivation. The ego part of our minds wants us to see differences instead of equality. It wants us to be unfairly treated and to forget that God created us equal, and that we are all innocent Sons of God in truth. Some of the forms of this kind of forgiveness are more obvious than others, but they all lead to imprisonment of the self. One example of this kind of forgiveness is when you find yourself forgiving someone from the perspective of you being the "better" one, while still holding on to the grievance done to you by the other. You can't see someone both as the Son of God and a person who is evil at the same time. If you've already made it real, you cannot forgive it. Remember, as you see him you see yourself. Minds are joined. We are all equally the Son of God. You don't have to agree with someone's choices or behavior, but you don't have to judge or condemn a person either.

Another form forgiveness-to-destroy takes is the idea that you and another are both unworthy of love. In your mind, you share your sinfulness with another. In other words, you condemn yourself and see both parties as guilty. This cannot be true forgiveness. It can appear to be a humble thought at first, but this is not freedom. You are either both innocent or both guilty. Which one would you choose?

Another role we tend to play is the role of martyr. We want to be careful that we aren't pretending that we feel at peace when we in fact feel hurt. It is not being honest or authentic with ourselves. We carry the burden of suffering for others with a false sense of sainthood, yet still retaining the sinfulness of the other in the mind. That cannot be love, but it is sacrifice. When this happens, we are in need of healing, which we can do with true forgiveness as described above.

Another form that false forgiveness takes is bargaining and compromise. *I will forgive you if you meet my needs, for in your slavery is my release.*[10] When we think this way, we are imprisoning ourselves. When we attempt to rid ourselves of the pain of guilt in this manner, it only leads to more pain and misery. The only way to escape the pain of guilt is to recognize our need to hold onto it, the purpose it serves, and then let it go. The purpose of holding on to guilt is that we get to be right, making the whole thought system of the ego real. Guilt says that we are not as God created us. It implies a belief that we can oppose absolute reality. This is impossible. The best thing we can do with guilt is forgive it by forgiving our own projections onto others.

Anytime we feel unfairly treated, which is easy to do, we need to be gentle and patient with ourselves as we work through those feelings. When the above steps of true forgiveness are applied with as much meaning and motivation as you can give it, you will experience results as you continue to practice daily. Try and let go of the form your forgiveness takes, or what you think the outcome should be. Remember, we can't see the big picture and don't really know what would make us truly happy, but the Holy Spirit does. Trust Him to take your pain from you and translate it into forgiveness.

Quite some time ago I had a session with a medium, before I was into the Course and practicing true forgiveness. I was feeling unfairly treated in my mind by the fact that a particular person who was receiving lots of amazing information from Spirit wasn't sharing it with the world. The tone of my voice was one of frustration. I said, "I just feel there are so many secrets!" Spirit replied, "The best secrets are right under one's nose." Whoa! In my experience, that was one of the most loving ways to teach me a lesson in my feeling unfairly treated in that form! Spirit was merely showing me that I was pointing to myself as I condemned another or the world. I was "guilty" of the very thing I was accusing the world of. When I say "guilty" I don't mean we are really guilty in truth. I was coming from guilt in my mind, thinking I was right and knew what was best, instead of being understanding and forgiving. But what a simple, yet powerful lesson! Thank you Spirit.

The Dynamics of Projection

In order to heal ourselves, it is necessary to understand the meaning of projection, and the role it plays in the ego's strategy to keep us mindless. Projection occurs when the mind is entertaining a thought it finds unacceptable, and then attempts to get rid of that thought by project-ing it outside, making oneself mindless. We now conveniently forget we are the cause of what we don't want to see because it is now in some-one else. Ideas leave not their source, which means the thought that got projected out, which then produced an image, has not left its source in your mind. Projection makes perception. The Course explains that we first look within and decide at the mind level who we are going to listen to, the ego or Holy Spirit, and then either project or extend our thought. The ego projects fear and the Holy Spirit extends love. You can actively choose which part of the mind you are listening to by being mindful about how you are thinking in every given moment. Your mood will tell you which teacher you have chosen.

Since the projected world is already done and over, we can choose to reinforce the ego's script (the projected world) or switch to the Holy Spirit's script, which means looking at the projected world differently, with peace instead of conflict. That is our choice. The purpose of the world of perception is to keep us in a state of mindlessness. The Course says the world was made as an attack on God. This is convenient for the ego because it doesn't have to take responsibility for the pain of guilt, since it is now placed outside in someone or something else. This is only the case until we change our minds and become aware that we are minds and not bodies and we can look at things differently. Perception has blinded us in such a way that we have lost the true meaning behind what we see. We just accept what our body's eyes report without ques-tioning the deeper purpose behind things. The Course says about the body's eyes, *See how the body's eyes rest on externals and cannot go beyond. Watch how they stop at nothingness, unable to go beyond the form to mean-ing. Nothing so blinding as perception of form. For sight of form means understanding has been obscured.*[11]

I remember in my psychology classes how we were trained to listen and be alert for the actual meaning behind people words and expres-sions. Listening is an art, and takes quite a bit of practice. I can assure you your partners will appreciate the effort though! Most of us have lost the ability to truly listen to each other. The ego's voice is very loud and always speaks first, wanting to be right. **The better listener you**

are, the better forgiver you become. In my psychology classes, we were taught to listen on four levels:

1. **Listen to the content being shared**, and repeat back to the person what you heard.
2. **Listen for the meaning behind the content** as the words being used may not represent accurately what the meaning is that someone is trying to convey, and get clarification from the person if you are unclear of the meaning.
3. **Listen to the tone of voice as someone is expressing**, as they may say they are happy yet the tone has a melancholy feel to it.
4. **Listening at a deep level and being engaged**, looking the person in the eyes, not being distracted by externals; listening with presence.

Seeing and listening with correct perception just might save you countless arguments in your relationships, and will help you communicate better in the world in general. When we realize that what we see on the outside doesn't represent an accurate picture of the whole person, or even the world for that matter, it will motivate us to look deeper into the nature of a person or problem. Then, true understanding and compassion can replace the ego's need to control by assuming it understands what it sees. As soon as we assume we know, we stop learning. Jesus is trying to motivate us to be like the innocent child who asks what something means, not assuming we already know. Who do we ask? The Holy Spirit.

The reason why the Course is called A Course in Miracles is because Jesus wanted to give us an alternative perspective on the purpose of a miracle, shifting its focus to be more about the place of cause (mind) instead of the effect (world). This miracle happens when we shift from the ego's point of view to the Holy Spirit's, which gives us a much lovelier, kinder, and gentler interpretation of what we are experiencing. This is not a course in love, but removing the blocks to love. When we remove the blocks, love is just itself. Forgiveness helps us find and remove the barriers to love. The barriers are the secret dream in the mind, and the world's dream, which is a projection of the secret dream. The secret dream is the mind's dream of sin, guilt and fear. We believe that we have separated from God and are sinful because of it. We then felt guilty over the separation, and now fear God's punishment, which is just a projection of the ego mind onto God. The world's dream is a projection of the secret dream in the mind, which is the screen on which we project all our unconscious thoughts of sin, guilt and fear. These are the barriers to love. We can remove these barriers by forgiving these insane ideas, which is recognizing that nothing happened! Sin, guilt, and fear are made up concepts. We don't have to keep choosing that way of thinking. This takes lots of practice because we've been poorly taught by the ego over many illusory centuries that this world and body are our identity. According to the Holy Spirit, a holy use of time is that we use it for His purposes, learning our lessons of forgiveness which will lead us home to God.

Self-Forgiveness

Many people ask us in our workshops about self-forgiveness. Some say that they can forgive another person, but not themselves. There is so much guilt around this. All forgiveness is really self-forgiveness because there is only one of us, or one mind. **When you are forgiving another, you are automatically forgiving yourself, because you are not separate from the person you are forgiving.** It only becomes difficult when we don't believe we are truly joined. There is no separation between ourselves and our projections. With this mindset, you can remember that it's only hurting yourself when you don't forgive others. Self-forgiveness can be achieved through practice and asking the Holy Spirit for help on a daily basis, seeing yourself as God created you, not how you made yourself. If you practice the steps in forgiveness above with vigilance, you will succeed. Try to practice not letting your mind wander into oblivion. The Course says, *The correction of fear is your responsibility. When you ask for release from fear, you are implying that it* *is not. You should ask, instead, for help in the conditions that have brought the fear about. These conditions always entail a willingness to be separate. At that level you can help it. You are much too tolerant of mind wandering, and are passively condoning your mind's miscreations.*[12]

Anytime we are filled with doubt and uncertainty, Jesus is encouraging us to ask him if our choice is in alignment with his. If we are sure that it is, he says there will be no fear. If we are feeling fear, then we are not choosing perfect love. This is harder to practice in the moment of intense fear. The mind certainly can be trained to see and experience only love. It is a process that occurs over time, and from choosing the "miracle" over a period of time. If you feel it is hard to forgive yourself for something, practice looking at yourself without judgment. Look at the situation you are associating your guilt with, and practice being the observer of it without attachment. Just look. This is having a self-forgiving attitude. The last thing we want to do is root ourselves further in a dream of guilt. We wake up a little more each time we remember to forgive; to overlook the errors and mistakes in ourselves and others, which means we see all people through the loving, non-judgmental eyes of the Holy Spirit.

The Course says, *Forgiveness should be practiced through the day, for there will still be many times when you forget its meaning and attack yourself. When this occurs, allow your mind to see through this illusion as you tell yourself:* **Let me perceive forgiveness as it is. Would I accuse myself of doing this? I will not lay this chain upon myself.**[13]

This is another way of telling us that when we hold attack thoughts about others, we are really attacking ourselves since there is only one of us. We want to be mindful of what we are doing so we can change our minds to reflect the Holy Spirit's thought system. When we are attempting to point our finger at others, making them the guilty ones, we must ask ourselves why we want to hurt ourselves. Once we really understand what we are doing, we will extend love rather than project fear, and peace will return.

In summary, when all your forgiveness lessons are learned, you become a manifestation of the Holy Spirit, just like Jesus became. This is the real world. The wrong mind disappears, because there is no more guilt to project onto self and others; the right mind disappears, because it has corrected the wrong mind, and there is no more need for correction. You are a living manifestation of the Holy Spirit, and there is nothing more to choose between. You may still be in the world, but the world will look very different to you, not in form, but in content. Everything will be seen through understanding; through the loving and forgiving eyes of the Holy Spirit. Then, *Here you are led, that God Himself can take the final step unhindered, for here does nothing interfere with love, letting it be itself. A step beyond this holy place of forgiveness, a step still further inward but the one **you** cannot take, transports you to something completely different. Here is the Source of light; nothing perceived, forgiven nor transformed. But merely known.*[14] In other words, the Course leads us to what lies beyond words, to what is known. Our learning has ended, and we continue as we were before tiny tick of time was made. There is and always was, only God.

Page for Personal Notes

CHAPTER 3

USING YOUR EVERYDAY LIFE AS A CLASSROOM

The Atonement was built into the space-time belief to set a limit on the need for the belief itself, and ultimately to make learning complete. The Atonement is the final lesson. Learning itself, like the classrooms in which it occurs, is temporary.[1]

Today, as I write this chapter (March 20, 2020), the world is going through a major pandemic having to do with covid-19, or the corona virus. Since this chapter is focused on using your everyday life as a classroom, I thought it was appropriate to discuss the corona virus situation within the context of the Course. I don't think anyone would argue that this truly feels like "new" territory as the world seems to be drastically shifting before our eyes; that this has become a part of most people's everyday classroom. Life as we know it is different. By the time you read these words, things may have shifted to a more positive, upward trend. If not, or things appear worse, perhaps what I have to say about it will bring some comfort. Regardless, you can use the information and apply it to any situation that is upsetting you, and work your way back to peace.

As you read my commentary on the Course's perspective on problems below, if any of it seems insensitive, please have an open mind. A new mindset sometimes requires some spiritual background and experience until it becomes a part of you. If you start to feel uneasy, ask yourself the following: Is it insensitive to be as God created you; to be free of pain and suffering no matter what is going on? Is it insensitive to have a mindset where you can rise above the battleground of the projections of sin, guilt and fear, and reclaim your identity as Christ? Is it insensitive to reclaim your power to choose how you think about things? Things can certainly be experienced as traumatic, and I'm not here to deny that, or to dismiss anyone's experience or feelings. What I am presenting to you is another way of looking at things, even in the face of extreme circumstances. If you, personally, have been affected by the virus, perhaps some of these ideas can inspire a new understanding, with patience and love for the self.

Although the corona virus is looked at as a specific problem, the Course doesn't address specific problems because it says all problems are the same. It says, *There is no order of difficulty in miracles. One is not "harder" or "bigger" than another. They are all the same.*[2] This statement can be looked at as a correction for the ego's First Law of Chaos as explained in the Course, which is *the belief there is a hierarchy of illusions.*[3] There is no order of difficulty in miracles means that one problem in the world is not really bigger than another problem, because *all* problems are projections of the one problem of separation. The belief in the separation from God has taken the form of many problems, including financial, relationship issues, health, and anything else you can think of. This means that even the current pandemic is part of the projection of the one mind of the belief in separation, and it's no different than anything else, because it serves the ego's purpose in the same way other problems do; to keep us focused on the world, which has us forget we are minds and that our real identity is Spirit, not bodies.

The other statement above that says "the belief there is a hierarchy of illusions" means that we believe that one problem is indeed bigger or harder to overcome than another. The Course is teaching us that if we recognize the true problem, our belief that we separated from God's love, and bring that problem to its correction that says all our problems have been solved because the separation has been solved, then all the other problems we appear to have would simply not affect the peace of God within us. They may not disappear physically, but mentally. This means that you would experience peace regardless of circumstances because you understand that when you correct the only lack there really is (a sense of separation from God) then you have corrected them all. Please review the first chapter if you feel it would be helpful to go over what pure non-dualism means.

The corona virus can be used as a way of watching your mind wandering, which means you can monitor your thoughts and reactions to it. If you notice any sense of lack or stress, or upset in any form, that is a red flag that tells you that you can choose again how you are thinking about it. You can choose the Holy Spirit's interpretation instead of the ego's. You'll hear me repeat this phrase often, because this is our one, true power of decision. This can be practiced by first recognizing when you get upset, and look at it without judgment. Try being the observer without attachment to the event. Invite Jesus or the Holy Spirit to look with you, which means you are looking through the eyes of innocence, wholeness and love. There is an exercise coming up in this chapter that you may find helpful with anything that upsets you. It can really help you remember your strength and power of choice, the only thing we really have power over. No matter how hard things appear to be, it doesn't have to take away the peace of God within you.

The world's virus pandemic is a projection of the inner pandemic in the ego part of the split mind. What boosts the immune system of the mind, along with forgiveness, is being vigilant *only* for God. The ego *is* the virus. The greater lesson around the virus is *What is out of balance within the mind that is causing the effect of imbalance in the world?* How we treat the earth is a reflection of how we treat ourselves and others. Once we learn how to undo the ego, we are no longer at the effect of the body or world, and that includes any particular projection of that in form, including a virus. This means that even if you have the virus, you will experience it differently if you are choosing the Holy Spirit's perception, which represents the alternative point of view, and brings peace to your mind. True forgiveness, as discussed in the last chapter, is the tool the Course encourages in the undoing of the ego. Peace will return to your mind no matter what is going on when you accept the Atonement for yourself. This means peace can be possible in the world, because the world you see is in your mind. If you choose peace in your mind, you will experience the world with peace.

If you choose fear in your mind, you will experience the world with fear. You are free to choose.

There is no question that a world pandemic can affect all aspects of our lives in form. This is where it's wise to do the normal thing and do what you can to take care of yourself in the dream. However, at the mind level, you know that you can exercise that power of choice to choose the strength of God within you, trusting that your abundance as God created you is not limited in any way. If you are using any situation that disturbs your peace as a classroom to further your growth and understanding, then you are well on your way to freedom.

There is a section in the Course called the Manuel for Teachers. Number 11 in the Manuel asks the question: How is Peace Possible in this World? The Course says, *In your judgment it is not possible, and can never be possible. But in the Judgment of God what is reflected here is only peace.*[4] *Peace is impossible to those who look on war (remember how some are referring to the corona virus as a war). Peace is inevitable to those who offer peace. How easily, then, is your judgment of the world escaped! It is not the world that makes peace seem impossible. It is the world you see that is impossible.*[5] The world we see through our egos, with our bodies eyes, is not the truth. It is a projection of the thought of separation. Fear is made up by the ego as a defense against the truth. When we exercise the power of our minds to choose peace instead of fear, we will see a world that is calling for love. From this perspective, we can be more helpful as we turn over the specifics of what form that love will take to the Holy Spirit.

The Holy Spirit is the answer to whatever forms our problems take. The problems we made up aren't real. They will seem real as long as we choose to hold onto them, making them the cause of our reality. **This is the key: It's not that we shouldn't respond to certain problems or take action if necessary, especially in emergency situations, but we can respond while practicing remaining in the calm center as much as possible, and remember that is a choice we can make.** When we look at the world through the Holy Spirit's judgment, we only see peace because we understand that it's the only thing that's real. We overlook the body or world, which means our body's eyes may see the body or world, and even chaos, but in our minds we think of it differently. We see only Christ everywhere, whole and innocent, and then if we are inspired to take action, we can do so from a calm centered place.

There may be times you find yourself reacting to circumstances quickly, and with fear. If that happens, just do your best to recognize your state of mind as soon as possible, and then you can change your mind about it when you are ready to say once again, "I want peace above all else." Remind yourself that peace is your goal. Ask the Holy Spirit for help. When you ask, it always produces a response. Trust that the answer will come to you in a way you can accept and understand, but let go of the assumption that you know what the best answer is. The Holy Spirit's answer is always for the highest good of all concerned. We can't see what is best for everyone, so it's best to trust the Holy Spirit.

Many people have turned to "conspiracy theories" to explain what may be behind current world events. There are certainly conspiracies in our world, but there are also some that may not be totally accurate. Gary and I get asked quite a bit about what we think about these alternative points of view. Although there is plenty of material to research and explore around this, and even what looks like some convincing evidence, I feel that if I start going into all the details of these things, it would be a great distraction from the Course's message of applying forgiveness. The point of the Course is that no matter what is going on in the world of dreams, no matter how big or small, or how insane it seems to get, it's *always* for forgiveness. This doesn't mean that if you are naturally interested or guided to do some research on other theories about the world that you shouldn't do that. Just ask yourself what purpose it is serving. Is it coming from fear and judgment, which makes the world real, or from a genuine interest? Are there unhealthy attachments to the people and events that you are researching? It's okay to be informed in our world. However, it can be done without any judgment of the people or circumstances you are reading about. At the end of the day, conspiracy or not, the work is still to look at your own investment in such things, and remember that if something you see is disturbing you, there is always another way to look at it.

There is great discussion on disclosure of all kinds of things that we may find out about in our illusory future. This dream may get even more exciting and dramatic. Even still, no matter what information might come to "light," always remember that you can stay in the "eye" of the storm if it is something upsetting. Forgiveness keeps you in the "eye;" the calm center. Also, whether or not some of these theories we are hearing about are right or wrong, the purpose we use them for is still the same; to forgive. It would be wiser to focus on the underlying cause, or root of any issue instead of the effect of whether something really happened or not in a dream. Furthermore, in the bigger picture of reality, nothing happened. That can be a mindset you have while still being helpful in the dream.

In these uncertain times in our world, the certainty of the Kingdom of God is what you can always count on, and never shifts or changes. **You are at home in God *now*, but this reality is obscure to you, because you have made another God in His place**. True Prayer, as discussed in the Course's *Song of Prayer* supplement, is a wonderful way to join with God's love. It is also one of the ways of undoing the ego, along with forgiveness and putting the Holy Spirit in charge of your day. I would like to repeat the exercise that I laid out in five steps on True Prayer that I included in my first book, which is a reminder of how to let go of the false god (the ego), which we've all made an idol of, and join with the true God, the God of perfect Love; the only reality that is real. Here is the exercise, which I recommend you do daily to help you return to a state of peace and calm:

True Prayer Exercise

1. Visualize taking the Holy Spirit or Jesus's hand and going to God
2. Lay your problems and goals, and idols on the altar before God as gifts
3. Think of how much you love Him and how grateful you are to be taken care of, forever safe and totally provided for.
4. Then, become silent with the attitude that God created you to be exactly the same as He is, and He wants you to be with Him forever.

5. Now, let go and join with God's love and lose yourself in joyful communion with Him.

Every time I do this exercise, I receive inspiration. In fact, True Prayer has proven to me to be a very helpful way to get answers. And the answers seem to be exactly what I need at the time. The Holy Spirit always knows. I let go of *how* the inspiration should come, and just allow it to flow through in whatever way the Holy Spirit knows is best. Trust that it will come, and stay open.

Let's review the idea that there is only one mind. As you join with God in True Prayer, the whole mind benefits. You are re-joining with what you really are, and the whole Sonship is included. As you think about other people, and are thinking thoughts with the Holy Spirit, you are reinforcing that strength within you and in the Sonship. If you are at the effect of the world, and buying into the fear of the ego, judging and condemning others, you are reinforcing fear in yourself and the whole Sonship. This is why your ability to exercise this choice is so important. The experience you have in the world will be a reflection of what teacher you have chosen, and you have the opportunity to reinforce love instead of fear; joy instead of pain; peace instead of conflict. **It may feel at times that the ego is dying, which can seem scary at times. Remember, it is literally fighting for its existence. This is because it thinks it *is* you. When this happens, try not to fight back, but remember instead that there is no death**. Death is merely a thought in the mind; a belief about yourself that keeps you afraid of awakening in God. It is also the last illusion we need to overcome. You dream that you are born, and you dream that you die. It is all a dream. The mind is mentally reviewing all of it, and the whole story of your life. Once this idea is accepted, it can literally change how you live in this world. There is no need to react with fear anymore. You can walk this world with the Holy Spirit instead of the ego. **There is no death, only life.** You always have "mighty companions" by your side, meaning those loving and forgiving thoughts that are available for you to choose at any time. This can bring great comfort when you remember this. A visual that is helpful for me is to imagine Jesus and another Ascended Master on either side of me when I am going somewhere. This reminds me that I am always safe with loving beings beside me. If you find it hard to visualize, just imagine it or think it into being. The fact that you are thinking it makes it true for you. I assure you that you have loving beings around you all the time. Trust it!

When thinking of ways to take care of yourself, let's not forget that laughter is a wonderful immune system booster! During this seemingly uncertain time of the corona virus and our changing world, a friend of mine sent me a joke to lighten things up a bit. It was an image of 3 extra-terrestrials, and one of them said to the other two, who were sitting on a couch drinking wine, "Hey Ladies! Whatcha up to?" To which they replied, "Watching season 2020 of earth, shit is getting wild!"

In addition to practicing forgiveness on a daily basis, how does one maintain a mindset of peace in a world that is literally changing before our eyes? For starters, recognize that this is a classroom for learning your lessons of forgiveness. It is a classroom for remembering we are One. It is a classroom for learning that we are all guiltless, and innocent in truth. There is no other worthy purpose for the world than this. Our only function here is forgiveness. Once we undo the ego, there will be a recognition that there was never really anything to forgive, because understanding will take the place of judgment. This happens when we reach the top of the ladder in which the Holy Spirit guides us. The "real world" is the forgiven world, and the choice between the ego and Holy Spirit is no longer necessary. You are only listening to one Voice, the Voice for God that speaks truth, the Holy Spirit. You have then become a manifestation of the Holy Spirit as Jesus did. Isn't that worth aspiring to? I think it is! All the masters throughout history knew it; Jesus, Buddha, Shakespeare, and more. You can do it, too! You can be a light that leads others through the dream of fear as you choose light for yourself.

I'd like to share with you a bit more of my life as a classroom, and how I was led to the Course, followed by some daily exercises and practical applications of the Course principles that I find helpful in times when my peace is disturbed.

I grew up in Toledo, Ohio, in the 70's when disco was the "hot" music, and bell bottoms were the fashion. As I look back, the 70's fashion was gentler to my eyes than the 80's shoulder pad shirts and "loud" eyeshadow! I often joke that I looked older then than I do now. I was always a musical child, taking piano lessons starting at the age of 4, and singing and acting lessons in my early teens. My family was very musical on both sides. At family reunions, which we would have every year, we would all sing, and my parents on both sides would sing four-part harmonies with their siblings. When I was really little, my mother would hold me in her back baby harness while she was playing the organ during her practice time at the church. I was developing a musical ear very early on, which would later help me with my music compositions.

Both my parents were very educated. My father, now retired, was a professor of American History and my mother (also now retired) was both a music professor and a psychologist. They divorced when I was 3, and my dad married an English teacher, who taught English to 8th graders. So, I had 3 teachers as parents growing up. Along with my sister, Jackie, I now had two more siblings entering the family, my step-brother and sister, Jeff and Leah. We were all close growing up and played games together, "hung out," and had many memorable family trips. Jeff passed unexpectedly in 2014 at the young age of 43. He will always be remembered as a talented musician and loving brother to me, as well as a very smart and genuinely wonderful guy.

I was very shy when I was younger, and didn't really enjoy talking to adults, except my own family members. I was a very observant child, and noticed everything. I remember being really interested in people's reactions to things, and even had a sense about people when something was wrong, although I didn't really express it openly. I didn't really have a lot of confidence growing up, although I excelled in all my activities, including sports, the arts (especially music) and got decent grades, with some minor exceptions. I always had friends, and had a pretty typical childhood in general. I also knew I would one day move to California, and get involved in the entertainment industry. I couldn't explain how I knew, I just knew. I recall a conversation I had with a friend when I was just 12 years old. I told her that I was going to move to California one day and become famous. I don't care about the idea of fame now, but at the time it felt very real. She looked at me in disbelief and said, "Really? How do you know?" I told her that I just knew, but couldn't explain *how* I knew. I knew I'd be in California. To me, that is a testament that our scripts are written and they just have to play out, but somewhere deep in our unconscious we know everything. We also know that the world isn't our true home, although we have forgotten that part. So, in 1987, I did end up moving out to California with my mother, and we started a new life there. A series of events unfolded that led us to the Course, which has been a big part of our path.

When I was 15, I experienced my first panic attack and thought I was going to die! My heart was racing, palms sweaty, and there was an overwhelming sense of doom or loss of control of my mind. When it happened, I was looking at a painting of Jesus ministering to the masses, and I had a visceral reaction to the image. I found out much later by a well-known medium, that it wasn't Jesus I was reacting to, but rather an unconscious memory I had of some of the more intense times of being around him when his life was threatened. I was told I was the disciple, Thaddeus, also known as St. Jude, in that lifetime. Please note: I'm not saying I am a Saint! The Church made Saints of all Jesus's disciples. Some of us disciples were threatened as well for being friends with him and spreading his true message, which was blasphemy to many who didn't understand the messages of non-duality Jesus was teaching at the time. Arten and Pursah, the two ascended masters who appear to my husband, Gary Renard, also confirmed Gary and I as the disciples, Thomas and Thaddeus. To me, this made total sense because I had many dreams and visions about Jesus growing up, and always felt I knew him beyond the "normal" feelings one would feel about someone. There was a sense of excitement when I would think about him, and I would find myself glued to the TV whenever a movie would come on about his life. The script called for both Gary and I to come together in this lifetime to continue spreading the true messages of Jesus from 2000 years ago. This time, we can do it without getting our heads cut off (like Thomas experienced and Thaddeus witnessed). I always got a kick out of Pursah's comment in Gary's book, "The Disappearance of the Universe," referring to her past life as Thomas (who is now Gary) when she said: "When you are in a body, you never know what kind of day it's going to be."

Note: Speaking of the disciple, Thomas, Michael J Tamura, who wrote the foreword for this book, is a "split" of Gary, and he also has memories of being Thomas. This is possible when you remember that since the mind divides and subdivides, there will be some people who have similar memories. Sometimes an individual soul has up to seven splits at a time, or possibly more, which means there are other aspects of your particular soul incarnate at the same time as you. Of course, in the bigger picture, we can remember that we are all aspects of each other, being of one mind, but we can experience ourselves as recalling memories being a particular personality at a certain time in our illusory history. Sometimes you meet them and sometimes the script calls for you not meeting them. In our case, Michael Tamura and his lovely wife, Raphaelle, actually married us in Hawaii. That is pretty rare, that a "split" of Gary married us. Michael is Japanese, but he and Gary still resemble each other quite a bit. They both have a love for music, play guitar, have a sense of humor, and are spiritual teachers. So it's interesting seeing them together! Personalities can differ a bit, of course, but in general some key characteristics remain the same.

To this day, one of my biggest forgiveness lessons, although not the only one, has been forgiving the panic attacks and related anxiety. After practicing the Course for over 15 years now, I have learned that anything we feel that is not love, whether it be depression, anxiety, worry, doubt, jealousy, etc. can always be traced back to the belief in separation from God. Practicing the Course will lead you to the highest state of consciousness you can achieve, being in the "real world" as I referred to earlier. The knowledge of God, which is beyond time and space, will return when you wake up from the dream of separation. If we can't acknowledge God, who is perfect love, and our only Source, the ego will be delayed in its undoing. If it is difficult to acknowledge God, it might be helpful to substitute perfect love in its place. God *is* love. All paths lead to God in the end, but the Course is a fast way to get there. The reason that is a nice idea is that the sooner we learn our lessons of forgiveness, the less we suffer. Jesus says in his Course: *Every minute and every second gives you a chance to save yourself. Do not lose these chances, not because they will not return, but because delay of joy is needless. God wills you perfect happiness now.*[6] We need to align our will with God's, remembering it is the same. We have dreamed that we have a separate will, and this is the cause of our suffering, the guilt over having believed our will can be separate from God's.

Over time, my anxiety has lessened as a result of my not judging it, which doesn't make it real, and the practice of true forgiveness. Even if it shows its face every now and then, I don't let it take away my peace, but just observe it with the Holy Spirit, and then let it go into God's hands, while doing whatever is necessary at this level to take care of myself. You can trust the Holy Spirit because it only knows the truth about you, as whole and perfect Spirit. What is helpful is remembering that the ego was not made by love, but was a projection of the belief in sin, guilt and fear. The Course says this about the ego: *Its evaluation of you, however, is the exact opposite of the Holy Spirit's, because the ego does not love you. It is unaware of what you are, and wholly mistrustful of everything it perceives because its perceptions are so shifting. The ego is therefore capable of suspiciousness at best and viciousness at worst. That is its range.*[7] All you have to do is look at the state of the world to see that this is so. The ego is never certain about anything. This has helped inspire me to be vigilant *only* for God. Only love is real, and everything else is made up and doesn't exist. There is no need to pet the ego and make it your friend. **The best thing we can do with the ego is *undo* it. Eventually, you will recognize that the "good" things that happen in the world are only good in relation to the "bad." They are both untrue, because they are not the love of God.** God's love is beyond time and space. It is non-dualistic in nature.

How I Found the Course and Met Gary

In my early 20's, I was starting to open up psychically and spiritually. I was having experiences that were showing me that I was more than the body. I was being prepared for what was to come: My study and practice, and eventually teaching A Course in Miracles. It was in the mid 90's when I first started noticing the Course in bookstores, and would take it off the shelf, flip through some pages for a minute, and then put it back on the bookshelf, totally *not* understanding anything I was reading. But…I was intrigued, and that is why I kept coming back to it and continued taking it off the shelf for another few minutes, and then putting it back. I have heard from many people that this was the same experience they had. Eventually, I just decided to buy a copy as I reasoned with myself that something was pulling me toward it. It sat on my shelf for another couple of years until one day my mother asked to borrow my copy. She had heard about it from some friends and knew I had a copy of it. She started attending a local study group. It was at her study group that she saw a copy of "The Disappearance of the Universe" lying on the coffee table. The facilitator of the group recommended my mother read it, which she did. She immediately started sharing with me about Gary and his experiences, and his funny way of delivering the message of the Course with Arten and Pursah. So, I picked up my own copy of the book, and read it. I found myself immediately drawn to Gary's personality, and felt like I knew him. Again, this wasn't the typical reaction of thinking you know someone, but more of a spiritual connection. The script called for us to meet, eventually get married, and teach the Course together.

Both Gary and I were married when we met, but our marriages were in their final stages. Steve, whom I mentioned earlier, was truly a wonderful man. We just weren't meant to have a life-long partnership. I am very grateful for everything I have learned from being married to him. It even came with some pleasant surprises, such as we also had known each other before in various lifetimes (although illusory) and his mother was a famous singer and actress (now retired) who even had a star on the Hollywood walk of fame. We were wed by the famous singer/actress Della Reese, and attendees included actor Kirk Douglas and author, Sidney Sheldon. Steve's dad was an agent (now retired) who had Barbara Streisand and Judy Garland as clients at one point. Through all of this excitement, I was still learning lessons, and even had what I would call a nervous breakdown in the early 2000's. Whenever I sensed an important change around the corner, I had a visceral reaction to it.

Eighteen months before I met Gary, Steve and I were about to make a big move to Michigan where he got a job offer. I loved California, and a part of me didn't want to leave, but another part of me was welcoming the change. Even still, I had an intense, anxious reaction to the move at first, and I went through a spiritual cleansing of some sort. It wasn't a pleasant experience because the anxiety kept me from venturing outside for longer periods of time, and I had all kinds of body reactions and twitches going on. One day, I was walking into our living room, and I almost collapsed because my knees were shaking and I felt a rush of energy move through my body from head to toe. I had to sit down and just move through it. Later, I was reminded in the Course that unconsciously we fear change because the separation from God was the first change we ever appeared to experience. I believe that my reaction to this period in my life, which was about to take a big turn and set myself on a whole new path, was more about the lessons I needed to learn — that I was not guilty over the separation — and that I could use the situation for my spiritual growth and learning.

Soon after Steve and I moved to Michigan and got settled there, the anxiety tapered off. We ended up staying in Michigan for 18 months before I moved back to California. I had just met Gary in Las Vegas before that, and there were many signs that it was time to end my marriage with Steve and embark on my new journey with Gary. Gary, who was married to Karen at the time, also felt the same, as his marriage was also coming to a close. Gary and I met at the exact time we were supposed to meet. There are no accidents. So, needless to say, this has been an interesting journey! In truth, what really matters is that we are using our lives, whatever form they take, for the practice of undoing the belief in guilt through forgiveness. This is what our relationships are for.

In light of what I discussed above regarding the corona virus, as well as all the issues we experience in our relationships, I have come up with a series of steps one can take to help deal with a situation calling for help, or whenever you get upset. Sometimes it takes a series of thoughts to work our way back to a peaceful mind, without blaming ourselves or another person. It also requires patience and determination to do the work necessary to train the mind to think differently; that is, shifting our perceptions where our grievances are replaced by forgiveness. No matter how difficult it may seem to change your mind, with practice you can do it. You can record the following steps in your own voice, and use it as a meditation if you'd like, or simply write them down and then take the time to ponder each step you reading. I hope you find it truly helpful.

Daily Exercise for Dealing with an Upsetting Situation

1. Invite the Holy Spirit to look at the situation with you, and find the quiet center within you. To find the quiet center, imagine yourself sinking downward and inward, moving toward the center of your being until you feel a sense of peace.
2. Acknowledge your feelings from this quiet center, and if you are still experiencing resistance, equate those feelings with the ego and remind yourself that the ego is not you, and it is understandable you would feel this way if the ego has been your teacher. There is another way to look at this. Remember, you don't have to be perfect, but your mistaken thinking with the ego can be corrected through forgiveness.
3. Let go of all judgments and assumptions that you know how to correct a problem, or even know what the problem is.
4. Say in your mind: Holy Spirit, please help me to perceive this person or situation with your Vision, not my own.
5. Remind yourself that you are never upset for the reason you think.
6. Ask yourself if you are willing to accept the Atonement for yourself. This means that you are recognizing that you are dreaming a dream and that its contents are not true. Nothing happened and you are still innocent, because the separation from God never truly happened. It just takes a little willingness to take it to the next step.
7. If you are willing, practice the feeling of gratitude for this opportunity you are being presented with to use it for healing. You might say to yourself: "Holy Spirit, please help me to use this

situation to facilitate peace." If you are not willing to feel grati-tude and are still experiencing resistance, remind yourself this is your decision, and when you are ready you can decide otherwise. At least you can decide you don't like the way you feel now. Then pause until your mind is ready to go further.

8. Trust you will be directed how to use the body with love instead of fear.

9. Pause…and wait to act on anything until you feel inspired, which means it will feel effortless, guided, and without force.

10. Let go of the form in which the answer comes or any results from this process. The fact that you even made an attempt to change your mind means the Holy Spirit is entering your mind, and you are aware there is another way. That is a great start!

I have found that it is so much easier to not push against the ego, trying to convince or change people and the world; rather, accept truth, or as I've explained earlier, accept the Atonement for yourself. You can look at the insanity of the ego thought system, but practice not judging it. When you forgive with non-judgment, the change will come as a natural extension of choosing the Holy Spirit. To further our understanding of forgiveness, the Course says, *To forgive is merely to remember only the loving thoughts you gave in the past, and those that were given you. All the rest must be forgotten. Forgiveness is a selective remembering, based not on your selection.*[8] This means that when we hold a grievance or judgment about someone, it is *our* selection. When we give it to the Holy Spirit, he tells us that the grievances we hold are not *His* selection, but here is what we could notice instead, giving us another interpretation.

A prayer by Cardinal Newman is relevant to this thought process: "And as they look up, let them not see me, but only Jesus (or the Holy Spirit). When people hear us speak, let them not hear us, but only His words." When we ask Jesus or the Holy Spirit to be our eyes through us, we can demonstrate to others that what they have done has not affected the peace of God within us. Another example of this would be the corona virus doesn't have to affect the peace of God within you.

This, in turn, reinforces your right mind and leads you further on the Atonement path. The Holy Spirit can't take away your lessons, but He can inspire you to choose the right teacher, to make the shift from the ego to the Holy Spirit.

Every day I wake up with the awareness that I'm dreaming, and that my life is a classroom. My daily practice is that I see the world but my awareness is above the world; above the battleground. This means that I am the observer of my life without judgment. I look with Jesus or the Holy Spirit at everything that hurts me, being really honest with myself with this, and remind myself with His help that I can change my mind about *how* I see the world. That is my power. This puts me at cause, so I don't have to be at the effect of a world that really isn't there in the first place. I am the author, writer, and director of my script. I can choose to watch my script play out with the ego, which reinforces the illusory dream, or with the Holy Spirit, who teaches me that the dream isn't true; that it was all made up by me, including all the figures in the dream. I make them act out for me by my interpretation of what I am seeing. I can always change teachers if I don't like what I am seeing. I can remember the truth. The separation from God never occurred, and is not occurring now.

We live in a world where technology, I believe, is once again exceeding our spiritual advancement. One way to rectify this is to think of mind as the ultimate technology. Even technology as we think of it in our world is made by the mind. Mind itself is the power, and we can use it for a holy purpose. This is the shift that needs to occur. The ego wants us to forget that we are minds, and that mind is cause, for the sole purpose of keeping the love of God out of our awareness. You don't have to be tricked by the ego. You can remember the truth and use everything in your daily life for the purpose of awakening from the dream of separation.

Have you heard of a TV show called Candid Camera? It was a well-known American hidden camera reality television series. The show used hidden cameras filming ordinary people, and sometimes celebrities, being confronted with unusual situations, sometimes involving trick props. It would put people in awkward situations. When the joke was revealed, the person was told the show's catchphrase, "Smile, you're on Candid Camera!" This is how I think of the world. When we wake up from this nightmare, it's as if someone will say, "Smile, this was only a dream!" We are just tricked into thinking we are really here, walking in a world of time and space, with props and backdrops, and all our senses which makes the world *seem* very real. Yet (for a quick review) the Course tells us the world was over long ago, and we are just mentally reviewing that which has already gone by. The ego came up with the greatest illusion of all time…time itself!

Our guilt over the separation, which we've taken very seriously, keeps us walking on the carpet of time, and forgiveness of the guilt awakens us from the dream of time. We simply forgot to laugh at our made up, insane ideas. Anytime we find ourselves getting caught up in the world, it might be helpful to remember, *It is a joke to think that time can come to circumvent eternity, which means there is no time.*[9] **Laughter is healthy, and I think of it as a tickle in the mind, reminding us not to take ourselves and the world too seriously**.

In light of the corona virus, I have been washing my hands much more often, probably like most people, because why not? It's the practical thing to do. Every now and then I allow myself to chuckle as a way of reminding myself to lighten up at the same time. In other words, I enlighten myself in that moment instead of getting too serious. Another way to stay in peace if there is a "storm" raging around you, whether it's a mental or physical storm, is to practice staying in the "eye," or the calm center. When you are in the calm center, you will experience safety and peace. You may want to practice finding your center through meditation until you truly feel you've found it. This way, if something pops up, you will be quicker in your ability to go there whenever you choose. In a sense, you are always in the center, but the ego has dominated your mind to the point where it is forgotten. In the next chapter, I will be including more exercises on how to relieve stress and anxiety, so you can reclaim the center of your being, your true Self.

Speaking of meditation, a guru was sitting with his students having a discussion on meditation, and a student raises his hand and says, "I'm meditating on my inability to meditate due to the fact that when I meditate I can't stop thinking about how I can't meditate, because I'm thinking about my inability to meditate. Is that correct?"

Another way we can help ourselves and connect to God is to help others. I heard someone say once, "Be a rainbow in someone's cloud." To be able to give love to others, we have to "be" it in ourselves first. When we are *being* love, we don't have to seek it. The love will naturally extend through us and be helpful to others. We just need to let go of outcomes. The form your love takes and how it is received is none of your business. When you are coming from your right mind, you will naturally do or say what is most loving. **Remember, try to let go of any outcomes you think need to happen as evidence that you extended your love to someone.** The same thing applies to forgiveness. When you expect someone or something to change in a specific way as a result of your forgiveness, it is the ego's way of trying to control the event. This always leads to disappointment. A good exercise is to practice listening to people, without judging them. Take a pause before, during, and after a conversation. Give yourself a moment to understand what the person is trying to communicate to you. When you allow this to happen, your response will be natural and without hostility.

Many people ask me what I specifically do to apply the Course in my everyday life. This is what I do: The moment I get up in the morning I put the Holy Spirit in charge of my day by saying, "Holy Spirit, please be in charge of my day today, and my thoughts and my actions, for I would follow you, certain that your direction gives me peace. Today, I make no decisions by myself." Sometimes I take it a step further and remind myself that I want to experience peace above all else, the joy of God instead of pain. I remind myself to allow the Holy Spirit to use my body for its purposes. Then, I sit outside for a little while on my balcony and I join with God in True Prayer as I described in the exercise above. If it's sunny, I imagine the sun being the light of God shining around me and through me, and bathe in the warmth with gratitude. I sit in this space until I feel a sense of peace wash over me. Throughout the day, I remind myself that I am dreaming no matter what is going on. It's all the same. If I am excited and happy or feeling down, it's still the same. It's all a dream. It is not the love of God. This helps remind me that God is all I want. I have no Gods before Him. This reminds me of something Jesus says in His Course, *There is nothing about me that you cannot attain. I have nothing that does not come from God. The difference between us now is that I have nothing else.*[10]

Jesus is telling us that we have the same potential to choose this for ourselves as He did. This also describes what it means to have an attitude of vigilance only for God. What are we investing our faith in? We can either be wholly devoted to the ego or God, there is no in between. It's one or the other, and we have to choose. Whichever one we choose is, in that moment, what we believe ourselves to be. This doesn't mean that if you choose the ego that you should feel bad about that. You can always choose again. You have all the time in the world because you are an eternal being. You will never run out of time! You don't have to suffer, and that is what choosing the Holy Spirit's interpretation (over time) will prove to you, that you can be happy, even in a mad world of dreams.

Finally, my daily practice ends with a statement I make to myself before I go to sleep at night. Since all my time is spent in dreaming, I put the Holy Spirit in charge of my night-time dreams, just like I do in the morning when I wake up. I say, "Holy Spirit, please be in charge of my night-time dreams, and my thoughts and my actions, for I would follow you, certain that your direction brings me peace." I trust that I am always taken care of and that the Holy Spirit is working with me behind the scenes to help me undo as much guilt as possible. I have to show up and do my part by being willing to turn things over to Him, not assuming that I know what is best in any circumstance, and then the Holy Spirit will do His part. The next morning, I start again with the same ideas in my mind and practice them through the day. I don't go around looking for things to forgive when things are going well. I just notice the times when my mind is wandering into the ego's world, and then practice changing my mind about it, seeing once again through the Holy Spirit's judgment instead.

I hope that by sharing my daily practice that it will encourage you to stay vigilant only for God. The form of your practice may be different. You may choose different quotes from the Course, or start and finish your day a bit differently, it doesn't matter. Just follow what resonates with you the most, and helps you to connect to the Holy Spirit. People often ask us whether it's okay to use the symbols of the world to help them connect to the Holy Spirit, such as angel cards, incense, music, nature, etc. There is nothing wrong with using symbols if it truly helps you connect to the Holy Spirit and God, remembering the truth of your oneness with Him. Symbols can serve a Holy purpose because they are giving you permission to be as you really are in truth. They are like stepping stones to help move you to the next level without fear. This is perfectly okay. If you start to become attached to the symbols by making idols of them, as if they have a power in and of themselves, then you may be falling into an ego trap, so just be aware of what you are using them for. They can be lovely stepping stones leading you to be more aware of love, but they shouldn't be confused with the love of God, which knows no symbols or form of any kind. Love is abstract.

I am a musician, so I often use music to inspire me to connect to God. I do this through singing, listening to songs that uplift me, and also through playing my Djembe drum. Gary always gets a kick out of it when I play it. He says I become possessed! In a way, I do become possessed. What happens is that I get in such an altered state that love just flows through naturally. This is what happens when there are no blocks to love. Music can assist me with this, just as for you it may be something else. Anytime there are blocks to love's presence it's because we aren't allowing the love to extend through us naturally. The grievances and judgments we hold about ourselves and others are marinating in our minds and dominating our thoughts until we notice them, pause and see them differently, and then let go without judgment.

It's easy to fall into egoic patterns of thinking (i.e. patterns of judgment) because the patterns themselves are reinforcements of the ego to maintain its position to exist, or be right. The pattern is a somewhat neurotic way of giving us the illusion that we are bodies. We have an unconscious need to prove over and over that we are a separate and special self, apart from God. When something comes up in our lives that really breaks the pattern of how we are used to living, such as a "natural disaster" of some sort, or even a pandemic, another way to look at that is that it can serve as a kind of intervention for ourselves to help us become aware of our own addictive patterns, no matter what form they take. It encourages us to look at our habits which make them more visible, allowing us to shift from the experience of being compelled to act without control to the awareness that we have a choice. We may even find ourselves having learned a powerful lesson, one that we can carry with us to help us make decisions for a more loving experience in our daily lives moving forward. In other words, perhaps we are learning that every experience we have can be helpful if we are using it to grow, heal and learn.

Perhaps you don't yet think that patterns can be changed, but they can! You can be just as vigilant to reinforce the right part of your mind as you are with the wrong part of your mind. Any time you feel you are stuck in a destructive pattern, remind yourself that if your mind caused it, then it's also in your mind to undo it. **The only pattern we really need to heal is thinking with the ego, and how we choose it over and over. When that is healed, all other patterns will heal.** You can make this a part of your daily practice by remembering that you can use your everyday life as a classroom in which you are learning that you are innocent and have never left God. In your conviction with this, you are demonstrating to others and giving them permission that they can choose the same. You don't even have to do anything specific, but correct your own misperceptions, which *is* the miracle, and is natural. With conviction, you will succeed.

Page for Personal Notes

CHAPTER 4

DEPRESSION AND SUICIDE: STORIES OF SURVIVAL AND HEALING MENTAL PAIN

The world you see does nothing. It has no effects at all. It merely represents your thoughts. And it will change entirely as you elect to change your mind, and choose the joy of God as what you really want.[1]

As I was sitting down to write this chapter, which will be the longest, I genuinely expressed to the Holy Spirit my desire to be truly helpful. I'm responsible for the words I write, but I realize I am not responsible for how it is received. So I let that go into God's hands, for He knows what is best for the highest good of all concerned.

I've known for quite some time that I wanted to write about depression and suicide, because I have always been aware of the silent suffering that goes on, perhaps because I am an empath. I pick up on the emotions of others. This is slightly different than being a psychic, who is empathic, but can also pick up on specific things about people's lives, or high probabilities of what might happen. My intuitive capabilities are experienced more as feelings, which are a form of clairsentience, or the ability to feel or sense subtle energies around myself or others.

I'll never forget when Gary and I went to hear a friend's band play. The following experience I'm writing about had nothing to do with the band, as they were a great band. It had more to do with the energy of the venue. I remember walking in and immediately feeling a sense of doom. Everything about the place smelled of darkness. I looked around and it seemed I was the only one who noticed or felt anything. Even the walls were a very dark blood red, and chipped, and the art on the walls seemed demonic in nature. Before we even walked in to the room where the band was playing, I said to Gary, "I have to leave, I just can't stay here a minute longer." I started to feel a suffocating sensation, and felt I was gasping for air. This is very rare for me, to feel that I have to leave a room because of the intensity of the energy. Even Gary admitted that it felt "dark" and he also wanted to leave. So, we exited politely and quietly, and once we got outside my breathing returned to normal. Gary said something like, "This is the kind of place where someone could be plotting a murder." Sorry to be so graphic about this, but this is an example of how important it is to pay attention to your intuition, or as some say, "vibes." You don't have to make a big deal out of it to those around you, but you can quietly remove yourself and explain your actions later, if necessary.

One could argue that, if you are a Course student, you should just be able to physically stay in the situation and change your mind about it, which would produce a better experience. This is always true at the level of the mind, that you can change your mind about anything and experience peace. However, one can do that, and still be guided as a reflection of choosing love in your mind to remove yourself from a situation that could be potentially harmful or dangerous. It isn't very loving to ignore one's intuition and pretend that things are okay when you feel they aren't. So, it's okay to take action and do what is necessary and then practice forgiveness as soon as you have a moment.

The reason I bring up this story is to encourage you to stay tuned in and to follow whatever natural guidance is coming through you, regardless of what others might perceive or believe. Perhaps you notice something about someone's behavior that seems "off" even if others don't see it, and you talk to the person and then discover he/she was feeling depressed and was planning on committing suicide. But since you followed your intuition, it produced an experience where you were able to talk to the person and give them an outlet to speak about their pain.

This also may be a cliché, but when you are walking along and smile at someone, even if they don't smile back, keep smiling! Kindness is under-rated. We simply do not know what other people are going through, and that maybe your smile helped them to trust that people can be kind, and perhaps that experience changed that person's mind about taking their life. **Always side on the position that you don't know.** If you find yourself reacting with judgment because someone didn't smile back at you, that just means that you were also in your ego mind or else you wouldn't have reacted that way. The Course puts it this way, *If you point out the errors of your brother's ego you must be seeing through yours, because the Holy Spirit does not perceive his errors.*[2] **For a brief review, this is how we forgive. We overlook other's errors in our minds, and remember that we are one. If you attack another in your mind, you are really attacking yourself. If you think loving thoughts about another in your mind, you are giving love to yourself. Remember, there is no cause outside of you. You are the author, writer, and director of your dream. You can interpret your dream any way you like, but attack leads to suffering and forgiveness leads to peace.**

Through the many years of doing our workshops, we have often come across people who have expressed to us that someone they cared about committed suicide. In some of the cases, it is they themselves who thought about taking their own life, and sometimes it is someone they know who is thinking about it, but hasn't attempted it. Whatever the case may be, taking one's own life, and even thinking about doing it involves a great deal of pain that is buried in the unconscious mind. Although the pain may appear to have a cause that is observable in one's life, the pain has more to do with the terrible guilt that can be traced back to the belief that we have really separated from God. That thought, which got projected out, now takes the form of feeling we lack something, and that something is God's love. Sometimes the thoughts we have are very conscious, and we can pinpoint what we think it is that is disturbing us. Underneath, though, there is a lot of fear taking the form of depression and anxiety that represents the ego's thought system of sin, guilt, and fear over the separation. There is no doubt that the ego can be vicious, and can dominate your thoughts if you let it. However, the good news is that no matter how "bad" things seem to get, you have a powerful mind that you can use to your advantage.

Depression

When it comes to depression, it definitely has a role to play in suicide. In all the stories I have heard from people who thought about suicide, depression was always a factor. The knowledge about depression, along with treatments for it, are more widely known now than in the past, which is good news. I do believe that getting treatment for depression as early as possible would most likely help prevent some suicides. Also, the importance of having a consistent thought system to practice, or faith of some kind can be tremendously helpful in keeping the mind focused toward the direction of healing.

Of course, sometimes a combination approach to treating depression and suicidal thoughts is necessary, such as taking a form of medication that can help one to function in the world more easily and without unnecessary suffering. At this level of the dream, we may have chemical imbalances that contribute to depression and anxiety (although not being the cause) and it is wise to pay attention to it and talk to your doctor if you think some form of medication would be helpful. Whatever one decides to do is one's personal choice, and no one is in a position to judge what is best for someone else.

Regarding the mind's role, if the depression is really intense, one might say, **"I don't have any motivation to change my mind." If this is the case, please consider the idea that it is impossible to lack motivation. The motivation is always there, it is what we are choosing to focus on that is the key. The mind can be trained, and that is great news!** I think it's helpful, as a Course student, to remember that if the body is in your mind, then anything having to do with the body, including chemical imbalances is still part of your mind's dream. Therefore, it can be helpful to keep that in your awareness, even if you do take some form of medication. Perhaps the medication is helping you to accept the healing in a way that keeps fear at bay. It's okay to use a combination approach if that is your guidance. Of course, it is always important to be kind, gentle, and patient with yourself. Whenever I feel pain or sadness in any form, it helps me to remember that I am dreaming the pain or dreaming the sadness. This helps me remember I'm still at home in God and never left Him.

I understand how devastating depression can be. I understand what it feels like to not want to get out of bed in the morning, or take a shower, go to work, and even to focus on anything in general, as even that can feel exhausting. I experienced the intensity of feeling that way for a two week period when I was on medication for anxiety back in the 90's. It was awful. That two week period felt like two years to me at the time. So I understand the deep sense of doom one can feel, and it's rarely helpful for someone to just say, "Hey, get up and get out there! You'll feel better!"

What my intention is in this conversation is to provide another way of looking at these moments that can feel so terrible by suggesting a viewpoint that comes from outside the ego system. If one is totally identified with the ego (like I was at the time I experienced my depression) then it would naturally follow that my experience would reflect that choice. I learned later that I have an alternative choice as to how I interpret the unhappiness I was experiencing. The alternative is listening to the other voice in your mind, the Voice of the Holy Spirit. That is very empowering, and I will elaborate on this choice later in this chapter. Someone once said, "You need nothing to be happy, you need something to be sad." Sadness comes from believing we are lacking something, and if the world is where we are seeking our happiness, we are setting ourselves up for being disappointed. We are seeking for happiness in the wrong place. Happiness is a state of mind that is inherent in what we are. We do need to choose it, because our goals are conflicted, and until we decide that our only goal is happiness, there will always be conflict.

If you feel hopeless, you can train the mind to start gently questioning that idea. You may want to remind yourself that hopelessness is not the end game. Hopelessness can be redefined in this way: It is the belief that the world and our bodies/personalities is all there is to our reality. If the world is based on separation, when we identify with this world and our bodies as our reality, then there is no hope because the world was not set up to work, and our bodies are a symbol of attack and separation, at least until we shift its purpose. Hope is still based on doubt about what you are. The *truth* about what you are is outside the system of time and space, and it's helpful to recognize this so that you begin to identify with the part of you that remembers your innocence. The truth about you, as you were created by God, remains intact. You can't be anything other than love itself unless you choose to believe that.

Before I get into actual stories of depression and suicide, I'd like to talk a bit more about another way of seeing things that the Course explains to us in regard to depression and anxiety, which can lead to thoughts of suicide. A more extensive commentary will also come at the end of this chapter. All this requires is that you have an open mind, without judgment, whether you agree with it or not. There is no need to persuade you of the truth about what you are and where you came from because ...*truth is real in its own right, and to believe in truth* ***you do not have to do anything.***[3] The more you undo the ego truth is simply there as it always was, because it is a constant. The Course says:

To identify with the ego is to attack yourself and make yourself poor. That is why everyone who identifies with the ego feels deprived. What he experiences then is depression or anger, because what he did was to exchange Self-love for self-hate, making him afraid of himself. He does not realize this. Even if he is fully aware of his anxiety he does not perceive its source as his own ego identification, and he always tries to handle it by making some sort of insane "arrangement" with the world. He always perceives this world as outside himself, for this is crucial to his adjustment. He does not realize that he makes this world, for there is no world outside of him.[4]

This statement comes back to the idea that we see the world we are choosing to see. There is no world outside because the world is an outside picture of an inward condition. If there is something in the world we think is bringing us pain, including our own bodies, it only means that we have made the world the cause instead of an effect. The world does nothing to us. It is the way we are interpreting it that makes it real or unreal; that gives it meaning or makes it meaningless; that brings us joy or pain. Once that is recognized you don't have to be a victim of outside circumstances. It feels better to reclaim your true power and remember that you get to decide how you feel.

The problem is that we have exchanged Self-love for self-hate. The Holy Spirit's evaluation of you is "wholly loving," because it is based on the truth about you, as God created you. We exchanged this love for the ego's version of love, and *its evaluation of you, however, is the exact opposite of the Holy Spirit's, because the ego does not love you.*[5] The ego secretly hates itself and feels guilty over the separation. We simply forgot where we came from, and so our perceptions are always shifting and changing. In other words, we aren't wholly dedicated and committed to the Voice that reminds us of our identity as God's one Son. Until we hear *only* that Voice, the ego will be suspicious at best and vicious at worst, as the Course says.

It is necessary to understand the strategy of the ego, before we can undo it. The ego wants us to feel pain, because this is its way of saying, "I exist as a special, individual self. I was right and God is wrong." Pain says the ego is real and God is not. But you are not your ego. You can identify with the right part of your mind, where the Holy Spirit resides, which is your memory of God. You are exactly as God created you. It is literally impossible for you to be anything else. This is good news! **No matter how much we resist love or forget that we are love, we can remember that love has not forgotten us!** God's love is unconditional and doesn't shift or change, regardless of the insane ideas we make up about ourselves and the world.

There is so much resistance to God's love, because unconsciously the separated mind believes that if we return to God, we will be annihilated over the terrible "sin" we have committed. Of course, there is no sin, it's only a belief. The resistance to choosing love is so persistent as reflected in the following statement, *Perhaps you are willing to accept even death to deny your Father,*[6] and then Jesus tells us how to rectify this by saying, *Yet this world (of death) is only in the mind of its maker, along with his real salvation. Do not believe it is outside of yourself, for only by recognizing where it is will you gain control over it. For you do have control over your mind, since the mind is the mechanism of decision.*[7] This means that once we recognize that all attack we perceive is in our minds, we can do something about it, because we have found its source. The answer to attack is also in our minds, and that answer reflects the Holy Spirit's interpretation of attack. All attack is a call for love. Once we recognize this, we can feel compassion for ourselves and others. This is so refreshing! We no longer have to feel like a victim. Victimhood is uninspiring.

Exercise of Inquiry

When tempted to let the ego's thoughts of fear (which can take the form of depression, suicidal thoughts, or anxiety) rule your mind, you might try asking yourself the following questions as found in the Course:

> *Do I desire a world I rule instead of one that rules me?*
> *Do I desire a world where I am powerful instead of helpless?*
> *Do I desire a world in which I have no enemies and cannot sin?*
> *And do I want to see what I denied **because** it is the truth?*[8]

Let's break these statements down one by one: The first statement means you can rule the world you see because you can choose *how* you perceive it. The world you see is in your mind, which means you are giving it the meaning it has for you. You always have that power. Once you recognize you do have a choice, you can practice not making the world or other people, or the circumstances of your life the cause of how you feel. The scripts of our lives are written, but not etched in stone. This means that there are various scenarios open to you, albeit within a "fixed system." One scenario is you choose peace, find your center, and remember who you are, which leads to "life." Another scenario is you choose fear and conflict, lose your center, forget who you are, which leads to "death." But you get to choose.

If you find yourself feeling so terrible that you are thinking of ending your life, or if you know someone who is, please remember and/or share with others the following possibilities:

Whether you feel like it or not, you are worthy of God's love, because He created you. You are an integral part of the whole Sonship.

Life circumstances can change! Think of a time when you thought something would go horribly wrong; yet it turned out not to be so. We never know what possibilities are ahead for us, because we can't see the big picture.

If you feel really "bad," it's both admirable and a sign of strength to seek psychiatric help through some form of therapy or peer support in a group setting.

Suicide is not really an escape, because the unresolved unconscious guilt one feels is still in the mind when one passes, and therefore you may find yourself reincarnating into a similar situation so you can learn more adaptive and positive solutions to problems. If one wants to escape from pain, it is escaped through awakening from the dream of separation, not through death. This can be done through practicing the kind of forgiveness as discussed in the Course, which I elaborate on in this book.

In the US, for extra help, people can call the National Suicide Prevention Lifeline: 800-273-8255

The second statement above is encouraging us to remember that we have a choice to claim our power as a mind that can choose how we feel and interpret something, or we can choose to see ourselves as a victim. Let's review Workbook lesson 31 in the Course: *I am not the victim of the world I see.*[9] This idea is reminding us that we are released from suffering as we free ourselves from the prison of our own minds. This idea, *I am not the victim of the world I see,* can be practiced by slowly saying this statement to yourself as a response to any situation that tempts you to think otherwise. The reason you are not the victim of the world you see is because you made it up. It's your dream. You get to choose *how* you see it. **Remember, the world does nothing; it is a neutral thing. It is our minds that give it the particular meaning it has for us, and you really are in control of your mind! You may want to review the subject of time in the first chapter regarding the world being over long**

ago. If the world is literally over, our only job is to choose how we are perceiving it *now*.

In order to be upset, you have to have duality. The mind has to be split. If there is no unified goal in mind, there will be conflict. If you want peace above all else, let that be your only goal, and the means will be given you to achieve that goal.

Statement three above is encouraging us to inquire more about what makes us suffer. Perhaps what is upsetting us is the belief we have "sinned;" that we are separate and different from others according to the ego's strategy of making people our enemies, and because of its judgment that there are "good" and "bad" people. Remember, the Course is telling us there is no world, which means there cannot be any people. In other words, we are dreaming of a world of duality where there are good and bad people. Comparisons kill. Comparison is an ego device that places us in a position of weakness and lack, especially when it involves the judgment that someone else has more than we do, or has something we lack. This belief is devastating to our minds and just breeds more guilt and fear. You have your own unique gifts to offer whether you know it or not. This is something worthy of being explored.

The Biblical line "Love your enemies" as supposedly said by Jesus can be reinterpreted this way: In truth, Jesus wouldn't say those words with the belief in His mind that He actually had "real" enemies, and is encouraging us to think the same. But since we believe we do have enemies, we need to forgive that in ourselves and accept responsibility for this belief. The idea of having an enemy is an interpretation we made that there are people trying to attack us. In the world, it can certainly play out that way, and I'm not here to deny that our bodies can be attacked; but we are *not* our bodies. If someone is appearing to attack you, remember that all attack is a call for love, as previously discussed. We could never perceive of someone attacking us unless we first made attack real in our own minds by believing attack is possible. I know that this perspective is totally different than what we've been taught to think or believe about the world, but that is why I trust it! Jesus is sharing with us this idea that the world, as made by the ego, is a complete lie! To experience a happy world, we are being encouraged to change our minds about it while we appear to be here. So the good news is that you can still enjoy yourself and have a happy dream of awakening by forgiving the dream world. And for clarification, if someone is physically attacking you, it's wise to do what you can to protect and take care of yourself, but you can still practice remembering that all attack is a call for love.

Finally, statement four above is asking us how willing we are to identify with the truth of God's love, which we previously denied. If we understand that we denied God's love as a defense to keep us mindless out of fear of God's punishment should we choose love again, then we can look (with Jesus or the Holy Spirit as our teacher) at our insane choice to separate from that love, and be reminded that there was no "sin." We are still innocent and at home in God.

These four ideas can become a part of your everyday attitude of forgiveness. Think of how important having a peaceful mind is to you. Even the act of committing suicide only means that you are attempting to find peace at the deeper levels because there is a feeling of loss. When you join in God's love, it will always replenish that seeming loss. **Peace is found through awakening *from* the dream of death, not deliberately dying in the dream thinking it will bring you "life." The world is not left by death, but by truth. So, we are awakening *from* the dream, not *in* the dream.**

Taking Responsibility for Our Thoughts

I trust that anyone reading this, up to this point, will keep in mind that the information being presented in this chapter (and the entire book for that matter) is being presented as a way to help people get in control of their mental faculties. In no way is it encouraging one to *not* take action if necessary, or if there is an emergency situation that requires immediate attention. The ideas being presented in this book are for the purpose of encouraging you to remember that the mind is where true change takes place, and the effect will take care of itself as we take responsibility for our choices.

Regarding taking responsibility for our thoughts, I was very encouraged when I read this from the Course:

> *This is the only thing that you need do for vision, happiness, release from pain and the complete escape from sin, all to be given you. Say only this, but mean it with no reservations, for here the power of salvation lies:*
>
> *I **am** responsible for what I see. I choose the feelings I experience, and I decide upon the goal I would achieve. And everything that seems to happen to me I ask for, and receive as I have asked.*[10]

This doesn't mean you are responsible for other people's behavior or thoughts. You are responsible for your response or thoughts about the world you see. No one is helpless in the face of all the things the world presents to us. When this is acknowledged, our mistaken beliefs in thinking we are victims will disappear. Your power of decision is yours to ignite! You are always choosing between the ego, which was a false attempt to make weakness real, and the strength of Christ in you. Whichever thought system you identify with is what you have made real. If you are choosing Christ, you are re-joining with your true strength as God gave it to you. Remember, we can forget this truth, but cannot obliterate it from our minds. Truth cannot be destroyed, only forgotten for a while.

Somewhere in our minds we all know the world isn't our true home. This may explain why we feel lonely sometimes, or sense that something is missing. We all have a buried memory of our true home with God, where we reside in His perfect love. The good news is that we can get in touch with that love here and now. It's not "death" that brings us back to this love, but awakening from the *dream* of death. As we awaken from the dream through forgiveness of our self and others, there are times that we may feel like an "alien" in our own homes or in the world in general. This can be a very persistent feeling. Everyone who is appearing in this world feels this to some degree, even if it's unconscious. This is why we endlessly search for things in the world to fulfill us, whether it be substances of some kind, seeking other's approval or validation in our relationships, or any "idol" we make of someone or something that we think brings us joy. The Course says, *A thousand homes he makes, yet none contents his restless mind. He does not understand he builds in vain. The home he seeks cannot be made by him. There is no substitute for Heaven. All he ever made was hell.*[11] This statement reminds us that we have chosen a "hellish" experience instead of accepting ourselves as God created us, in love, which is our true home. Nothing we have chosen here in the world can even compare with God's love. But we haven't truly lost our innocence, yet we yearn for it. Part of the practice of remembering our innocence is to see it in others, no matter who it is or what we think they have done. It is always a lesson in learning that you and everyone else are truly innocent, because none of us have really left God. It is only a dream.

Row, row, row your boat, gently down the stream…merrily merrily merrily merrily, life is but a dream.

I understand what it feels like to have low self-esteem or a feeling of unworthiness, since I experienced those feelings in my late teens and into my early 20's. You may even feel at times that you are the "elephant in the room" where people *should* "see" you, but maybe you feel that even if you stand as that elephant in the middle of the room, no one acknowledges you. What can help with this scenario is to remember that if you see yourself clearly and work on getting to know yourself as God created you (by undoing the ego), it wouldn't feel like a "sting" when others don't respond as you think they should. The idea is that when we are clear and certain about who we are as Christ, one Son of God, all the specialness needs we have become less important. Some days you may feel like wearing one of those "Do not disturb" signs around your neck. I've felt that way. We can be patient and kind with ourselves when we are in that space, remembering who we really are.

Personal Stories on Suicide

With the above context concerning how we can look at life and our experiences differently, I'd like to share a few stories of people I've interviewed who have been on both sides of the suicide spectrum. One story is of a mother whose son committed suicide at the young age of 20, and how she worked through it. Another involves a woman whose husband committed suicide and also how she worked through it. From another perspective, there is also a story of a man who attempted suicide, but changed his mind, and what led to that change of mind. For the purposes of privacy, the names have been changed. I thank the people involved for being so courageous in sharing their stories. The pain of suicide runs deep, and the process of healing is a struggle that takes time to work through, and sometimes a whole lifetime.

Sharon's Story

When I mentioned in a recent workshop that I was going to write a chapter in my second book about suicide, a very nice lady (whom I will call Sharon) approached me and gave me an envelope with a card inside. I read the card later that night, and she expressed to me that if I thought it would be helpful, she would be willing to share her story about her son who committed suicide at the young age of 20. In her words, "I feel it is very important to shine the light on suicide as it is not talked about." I was very grateful that she was willing to share her story for the purpose of being truly helpful and I accepted her offer.

Sharon is a mother of a son, Greg, who committed suicide when he was 20 years old. According to Sharon, Greg was handsome, smart, had lots of friends and a girlfriend, and went to a UC school. He was someone who, on the outside, represented the picture of a functional and well-adjusted young man. According to Sharon, Greg dealt with minor depressive episodes as a child, and off and on from there. Greg felt guilty as a child, not for any obvious reason, but Sharon mentioned an episode when Greg was very young. He came into the room with a pillowcase over his head because of the guilt he felt. One might question how a child so young could feel so guilty without an obvious reason. This brings up the idea in the Course that all of us are dreaming we are born with the ego intact, with guilt in the mind, or we wouldn't even appear to have the experience of being born in the first place. Sometimes the sense of guilt over the separation from God is so strong that we can feel it as children, even without knowing why we feel that way.

One shouldn't judge oneself or others for feeling guilty, since we all feel guilty, even if it's unconscious to us. We can educate ourselves. The more we are open to learning, the more aware we will become. We learn by always seeking for the truth, not assuming we know or understand anything we see, but accepting that we don't know what anything is for. This way, the Holy Spirit can lead us and teach us that forgiveness is the key to happiness, and that we can use our lives as a classroom for awakening from the dream of separation through forgiveness.

Although Sharon acknowledged that the family, in general, hadn't been good about communication, it is clear that the love was there. She and her husband always encouraged their son to get help along the way. They remained loving and understanding with him. Many families struggle with communication and lots of us grow up not being encouraged to talk about feelings. We shouldn't feel bad about this. We are learning lessons along the way, and everything that happens that disturbs us is for forgiveness.

As time went on, Greg's parents continued to encourage him to seek help from a therapist for the depression, and were doing the best they could with helping him through the depressive episodes. No one truly suspected the deeper struggle that Greg was going through. Silent suffering is something that goes on very frequently, and unless someone chooses to share what is happening, it's not always easy to read the signs. At one point, Greg said, "I wish I believed in something." But again, Greg just didn't seem like the type of person that would take his life, and after talking with Sharon, it seemed as if that would've been an unlikely scenario at the time. Afterall, Greg didn't even mention suicide until the last day of his life.

This idea about believing in something is very powerful. Gary and I often mention to people that whether it's the Course or something else, it is very helpful to have some kind of path to follow or thought system to believe in that you can turn to whenever your peace is disturbed. Again, it doesn't have to be the Course, but some kind of spiritual focus is so important. All of us are hungry for spirituality whether we know it or not. We are really hungry for God's love, but this is rarely talked about. Behind every act of violence or anger is a call for love. It is helpful to know this so that our response to a person's disguised call for love can shift to one of compassion, love, and understanding.

Soon after Greg started college he came home as a result of not being able to function. He was going through a major depression. After he came home from college with depression he went through a healing process. He was happy to be home again and be with his friends. He did some volunteer work and started a relationship with a wonderful young woman, which lasted for the rest of his life. Sharon and her husband still have a relationship with her to this day. Greg also finished his AA degree at the local college during this time. He transferred to the local UC campus and was doing well there. So Greg appeared to be balanced, mentally, for two years until just before he took his life.

The week before he took his life he had dinner with his parent's twice and seemed to be doing well. The weekend of his death, he came home on a Friday and told his parent's he was depressed and anxious. He talked non-stop with his mom, Sharon, all weekend telling her his feelings, which was a gift to her. He worked at his restaurant job 2 nights. He and his dad tried to track down his psychology teacher he knew to get an anti-depressant with no luck. The night before it happened, Greg was very anxious. Sharon held him and rocked him. He was afraid he was crazy. Sharon told Greg that night when he was telling her about all the things he felt guilty about that she wanted him to get counseling and stick with it.

The next morning, his father left on a business trip after Sharon assured him Greg wouldn't want him to stay home on his account. That was before Greg mentioned suicide. Later that morning, which would be the last day of his life, Greg said to his mom, "If I didn't love everyone so much I would take my life." I think one often defaults to the thought that "He/she wouldn't do such a thing," but Sharon took his statement very seriously, and that is why she had him see her minister that day as Greg continued to show signs of distress. Sharon learned, however, that if someone is determined to take their life, there is nothing you can do to stop them.

Sharon spent the whole day with him. She took him to church with her that morning, and they walked together with his sister on the beach. He saw the minister that afternoon at Sharon's request. After that, he went to a bridge where he had formerly learned of others who had committed suicide, and he jumped. He left a note that said, "If you loved me you will try to understand that this will end all my pain and misery."

Depression can indeed run in families. For example, Sharon explained that she had depression when she was carrying Greg before he was born. That continued a bit after he was born, and Greg also had some physical challenges after he was born, including pneumonia. Sharon was honest, open and courageous in telling this story, because she sincerely hopes it will help others to heal from similar experiences.

Needless to say, one should always deeply respect a family's process in healing after something like this happens. None of us can judge another's path, or how either one person or a whole family decides to recover from such a devastating loss. As Sharon described, the pain that the ones left behind feel is so devastating, and one goes through many different emotions, including guilt, shame, and anger. Even though this happened over 30 years ago, there is still to some degree, guilt in the family about Greg's suicide as it is sometimes very difficult for a family member to understand why or how this could have happened, and it's easy to blame oneself, and go over all the things you feel could have prevented it. Greg's father often feels he could have prevented it.

Soon after Greg passed, Sharon became devoted to improving communication in the family. In her own words, "The Course has been a tremendous help with that with all its insight into special relationships."

Coming into Acceptance

At some point, no matter how many times we go over what we feel we could have or should have done, it is helpful to come into acceptance of the situation as it happened, and finally forgiveness, which often (but not in every case) involves the following stages:

1. Denial or Victimization – we almost need to deny and feel victimized at first, which is the ego's survival tool
2. Anger – another defense mechanism or protective device against the pain one feels, which is really a call for love
3. A sorting out of the information – trying to make some sense out of what happened
4. Acceptance – coming to terms with what happened whether you understand or agree with it or not
5. Forgiveness – freeing oneself of the burden of guilt

The journey through these stages and feelings of discomfort often needs to happen before we can even consider what it means to forgive, which is to be able to see a different meaning behind things, an alternative perspective such as the one the Holy Spirit provides for us if we are willing. This involves the recognition that at the level of Spirit or reality, there is nothing to forgive, because cause and effect have been put in their proper place.

It is worthy of mentioning here that no matter how hard it is to deal with a loved one's passing through suicide, it is not anyone's fault. In Sharon's words, "Suicide of a loved one brings the ego's guilt we all have front and center. The death of a loved one by suicide is one of this ego life's most painful things to experience, but also it has been for me the most important "gift" and opportunity on my spiritual journey of accepting the Atonement for myself and sharing it with all my brothers and sisters."

We cannot control others or decide for them how they should think and feel. As much as we love them, no one is in a position to do this. Even if you did everything "right" in the relationship, it doesn't stop someone from taking their life if that is what they decide to do for their own reasons. Yes, it is painful. The pain is something that stays and lingers for a while, but the good news is that it can be healed with willingness, focus and forgiveness, and thinking about the good times and the wonderful qualities about your loved ones. Your loved ones are "alive" in a different form, in Spirit. They are still with you. They can hear you when you talk to them because all minds are joined. It is helpful to think of our loved ones as whole, innocent, and in God. This also helps them move on in their journey of healing. If we are one mind, then when we think of our loved ones in their wholeness, we are benefitting the whole Sonship, which of course includes ourselves. All of us are going to pass from this world, and the way one chooses to pass is not for anyone else to judge. It is an opportunity to forgive and remember the truth.

Sharon's Process in the Aftermath of Greg's Suicide

Before Greg's passing, Sharon had just started the Course, and had been into Religious Science up to that point. That really helped her on her spiritual path, and also to deal more effectively with Greg's passing over time. She did go through some depression that first year after he passed. Sharon said her healing is a continuous process in regard to the guilt she still feels at times. She is learning, especially, that this is a journey.

She sought spiritual groups for support, as the family didn't want to talk about what happened. To this day, her other son feels anger when it's mentioned. It is so important to be patient, kind and supportive of other family members, as they process what happened. In Sharon's words, "Greg's passing was like a rocket shooting me on my spiritual path to accept and deal with my feelings about his choice of suicide. My faith in a higher power, the spirit in me, and the eternal nature of life was my saving grace in my healing process. I was involved in counseling with my minister and teacher/mentor of ACIM (A Course in Miracles) for a long time. I very soon started working with young people of all ages who were in need of support in the issues of this ego life. As the Course teaches, giving is receiving, and I received a lot of healing from helping young people. I would tell people, 'Be kind to yourself, as the death of a loved one is like a wound to your mind and body. Get lots of rest, and be open to the love and support of friends and family, and eat healthy.' I found the exercise of walking very helpful. These are the things that helped me after my son's death."

Sharon also mentioned some specific lessons in the Course (listed below), which she still does, that helped her in healing for

those who may want to review these parts of the Course for similar purposes:

Lesson 47: *God is the strength in which I trust.*[12]
Lesson 41: *God goes with me wherever I go.*[13]
Lesson 137: *When I am healed I am not healed alone.*[14]
Lesson 162: *I am as God created me.*[15]
Lesson 50: *I am sustained by the Love of God.*[16]

These are the passages from the text that have been helpful to Sharon:

Your worth is established by God.[17]

The whole section on *Release From Guilt*[18]

All your past except its beauty is gone, and nothing is left but a blessing.[19]

The entire section on *Choose once again*[20]

In summary, an additional comment from Sharon is worthy of mentioning here: **"I dreamed of having the perfect marriage, family, and being a perfect parent, but came to the realization that "there is no such thing."**

When one seeks these things in the world, it is setting oneself up to be disappointed. It is not a practical goal. One can learn perfect forgiveness and come into acceptance of events that play out in one's life, but it does take time. One should be patient and loving with the self, and honor one's process of healing. I thank Sharon for sharing her powerful story, and for her courage and strength to bring up such a painful part of her past for the purpose of being truly helpful to others.

Debra's Story

Debra's story came to me in a similar way as Sharon's story. When I mentioned in another workshop that I was going to write about suicide, a very nice and pleasant lady, Debra, wrote to me that she would be happy to share with me the story of her husband, who committed suicide. I told her I would email her when I was working on this chapter, and when I did, she was so open and willing to share her story with me. I told her my purpose in sharing these stories was to be truly helpful to others who may be going through similar circumstances. I, too, believe that having a strong support system is key to how one deals with the aftermath of a loved one who takes his or her own life, as both these women I am sharing about have expressed.

Debra was married to her husband, Sam, for 25 years before he took his life. They also had a son. They did everything together and spent most of 24 hours together. They even bought an orchard together. Debra described her marriage as unconditionally loving. She and Sam always got along well, and truly enjoyed each other's company. Debra described her marriage as "joyful most of the time." When I asked about what might have led to Sam's suicide, Debra mentioned several things that may have influenced his decision to take his life. When I asked about his childhood, Debra said he had been sexually abused as a child by his uncle, and his brother had seen them together when it happened. Obviously, that would have been a devastating experience, and if one doesn't deal with the emotions of it, it will infest one's life with conflict until it is forgiven and released in one's own time. According to Debra, Sam didn't really want to talk about it. Then, to make matters worse, Sam was eventually diagnosed as HIV positive. Sam couldn't seem to accept that diagnosis. He saw it as a judgment against himself and couldn't forgive it. He felt like he was being punished. Sam resorted to using alcohol, and although Debra tried to reach him and be as helpful as she could be, Sam was in a "dark" place and seemed unreachable. Sam doubted himself and would say things like, "I don't belong to this world." One night he had to be hospitalized after being found in the car, passed out, which was the first time he had an episode of that nature. These episodes continued for a while.

Debra felt she was doing everything she could to try and help him, but at some point she realized she had to accept what was happening, and she knew she couldn't change his mind for him. She was loving him unconditionally, regardless of what was playing out in her experience. She never felt like leaving him, because that wasn't the answer for Debra. She committed to loving him unconditionally from the beginning.

As time went by, although Sam knew help was available, he didn't choose to seek that help in a consistent way. He started sleep-walking, and having episodes of memory loss, where he would wake up in a parked car in a state of confusion. He spent two weeks in a hospital, and when he came home, a few days before his suicide, he left messages in the house such as "I will always love you" and "I can't stand it any-more." He even came to kiss her good-bye, which really worried Debra, but she was doing all she could to try and help.

Debra woke up one morning and Sam wasn't there. She and her son, who was 21 at the time, went looking for him. They headed toward the barn. There was a note on the barn door that said, "My love, don't open the door, call the police." The door was locked. Debra's son was the one who got the door open, and he said to his mother not to come in, not to look, and so she didn't. Sam had hung himself in the barn. Debra never saw his body from that moment on, even at the funeral.

Debra's Process in the Aftermath of Sam's Suicide

I asked Debra how she dealt with the aftermath of this as she and her husband had experienced such a long life together and had been through so much. She described her process as one where it started with her self-medicating, followed by depression for one year. Before all this happened she had already started on a spiritual path after she was diagnosed with cancer, which apparently she got through. She stayed on her spiritual path, and continued reading a lot of material. She said that having that spiritual foundation really helped her in subsequent years in dealing with the death of her husband. Also helpful was a very supportive friend, who even called her the first morning after the suicide, and reminded her of God. Debra even found herself giving another friend messages of support, and realized it was for herself. She eventually started reading my husband's book, *The Lifetimes When Jesus and Buddha Knew Each Other: A History of Mighty Companions,* which helped Debra realize that Sam "left" for a reason. She was inspired to get more into A Course in Miracles which helped her "find herself." It was like "icing on the cake," as she put it. Debra said it was a process of about five years before she really felt more peace and moved into acceptance of the situation. She was really grateful that she had a thought system, a strong foundation from the beginning that helped her move through this very difficult situation. Even now, she is at peace with it all.

I asked Debra what advice she would give to others who may be going through the same thing. This was her response in her own words:

"Never feel guilty. You cannot intervene in someone else's choice. I realized I couldn't help Sam. I feel okay about it now because I forgave it. I never felt "he did that to me." The Holy Spirit knows, and I knew I had to follow His plan. The Holy Spirit has a plan and it was part of my journey, and I accept it as it is. I see it now in an impersonal way, from "Above the Battleground." Her final advice was to get professional help if you need to, and do what you need to do. It's always helpful to have friends who are supportive, and to surround yourself with them, but it shouldn't replace seeking professional help if needed.

Although Debra will always love Sam, it's quite remarkable that she doesn't miss him, because she has totally trusted in her path and in the greater plan of life in regard to her journey. I thank you, Debra, for sharing this powerful story of what is possible, even in the face of such trauma.

One should always allow the process of grieving to unfold in the way that is most helpful for that person. It is important to deal with the grief as openly and honestly as you can, and give yourself time and space to heal. At some point, when you are ready, it can be a very loving thing to start reminding yourself that there is another way you can look at this *now*. Your power is *now*. Even when a memory comes up, you can still decide to choose how you see it from your present perspective, through the eyes of forgiveness. You are literally a new person every second according to the choices you make, and so you can choose to see things in a way that reflects a willingness to keep growing, learning, and forgiving.

Many families just don't want to talk about their experience with suicide, or possibly feel ashamed because of what happened. I am hopeful that these stories are providing an outlet without guilt or shame for those that do need to talk about it.

Brad's Story

Brad's story is from the perspective of one who thought about committing suicide at the young age of 21, and then changed his mind. Before his first suicide attempt, Brad mentioned that he grew up in a family of alcoholics, and without ever having seen his biological father. He had always felt tremendous pain over that, and as a result felt very guilty. He did have a loving step-father, which helped, but the thought of not connecting with his biological father stayed with him. When Brad entered high school, he had a girlfriend named Sarah, whom he absolutely adored. He lived for this relationship and admitted the deep dependency he had on her. The relationship lasted for about five years. One day, Sarah abruptly ended the relationship, leaving Brad feeling completely devastated. In his own words, "I felt emptiness, and I couldn't take it. It was the worst feeling I've ever had." Brad's family owned guns. One day he got one of the hand guns and made sure it was loaded. He sat on the couch with the gun by his side, thinking about pulling the trigger. In his words, "I chickened out. I was too scared to do it, or maybe it was too much guilt and fear I was feeling of actually going through with it." That sense of hesitancy, in my opinion, could only mean that somewhere in his mind he knew there was another way, even if it wasn't conscious to him in that moment.

A year passed, and at age 22 Brad was still feeling the pain of being single. He started working in Paper Mills, among other things, and worked very long hours to numb the pain. He started to drink heavily. One day he got into a car accident as a result of falling asleep at the wheel. He ended up being okay, but that experience triggered his fear of dying. It also was the catalyst that inspired him to want to go home and read the Bible. As he read the New Testament, it helped him feel that everything was okay. He felt a connection with Jesus which, he said, "carried me."

When Brad turned 24, he was a Philosophy major, and still admitted to being suicidal. He saw a counselor for one year, which helped him work out some of the guilt he felt. **He also realized that what happened with his biological father had nothing to do with him. He was starting to free himself of some of that burden.** In Brad's words, "I remembered around that time that I realized never having seen my biological father had nothing to do with me. I started meditating every day (an Edgar Cayce meditation course to begin with). After six months or so of meditating every day, a general fear I had lived with all my life, left me. I have meditated every day since."

What "Saved" Brad from Taking His Life

Along with reading the Bible and seeing a counselor, Brad said, "The cure for me was finally coming to the place where I said, "I give up, and I surrender to you, God. I'm not in charge." Brad would kneel by the bed and pray in total surrender. He felt the light come through. Continuing to read Jesus's sayings really helped him connect with the Holy Spirit. Even then, Brad continued having some suicidal thoughts up until his mid 30's. He started practicing Rosicrucianism, which according to Wikipedia, is a "spiritual and cultural movement which arose in Europe in the early 17th century after the publication of several texts which purported to announce the existence of a hitherto unknown esoteric order to the world and made seeking its knowledge attractive to many. The mysterious doctrine of the order is "built on esoteric truths of the ancient past," which "concealed from the average man, provide insight into nature, the physical universe, and the spiritual realm." During that time, Brad also started studying and practicing A Course in Miracles.

When I asked Brad what advice he would give to others going through a similar experience with suicidal thoughts, he said what helped him is "Learning to listen all the time. Somehow the message has to come into the person's mind that giving up (or surrendering) is a good thing to do, but not from an ego perspective of giving in to guilt and fear. It's realizing that there is a wrong and right part of the mind and you can learn to be aware of which part you are choosing. Remember God, which is remembering your loving thoughts. Watch yourself having ego thoughts and practice changing your mind. That process furthers one's awakening."

An interesting part of this story is that Brad is now married with two young boys, ages 3 and 11, and the older boy has been having suicidal thoughts off and on for a while. When I asked Brad where he thought that came from since his son is so young, Brad courageously shared with me his thoughts, but without blaming anyone or defining one particular thing that could be the cause. As Brad knows from studying the Course, guilt over the separation from God is the cause of all suffering, although we don't always realize it because we forgot. Brad mentioned that while their son was growing up, there was conflict in the relationship between him and his wife, Carol, who happens to be a wonderful person, but they had some difficulties. Brad's wife was dealing with depression and would sometimes find herself saying around her son, "I want to kill myself." Later, John, the 11 year old, would start talking about killing himself, too. The son would tell his dad he was doing it to manipulate his mother. She would then give in and do what he wanted her to do. According to Brad, his son also sounds like he means it when he says he is going to kill himself. These are definitely signs to pay attention to and to seek for help.

Since the disciplining of their children has been a problem in the family, Brad shared with me that he felt he and Carol were still working on it, although it's been a struggle. The good news is that they have sought counseling for their son, and were told that anytime their son speaks of suicide they should take him to the emergency room, which apparently is a legal procedure one is supposed to take under those conditions. This is still a work in progress as Brad and Carol are dealing with the challenges and difficulties of their own marriage as well as how to effectively work with their son.

The point of this discussion is to emphasize the importance of bringing awareness to our conflicts so we can address them for the purpose of healing and growth. When parents start to address their own issues and work on their personal grievances individually, as well as together as a couple, it's a starting point for modeling for their children a healthy environment where they are able to express themselves in a safe and loving place and feel free to talk about their concerns and anxieties without the fear of judgment.

As I mentioned, Brad and his wife, who are lovely and sincere people, are doing their best to continue to be aware of their own issues, so that they can more lovingly seek the appropriate help and guidance for their son. Perhaps, as suicide often runs in families, there is a powerful "family lesson" being learned that is taking this particular form to remind us we are all innocent, and doing the best we can as we learn all things are for forgiveness of ourselves and others. We all share the part of the mind that is the ego, which breeds pain and suffering, and we also share the right part of the mind that remembers the Holy Spirit, that which is our memory of God, and that which we can choose to identify as our reality.

I want to thank Brad for being so courageous in sharing his story, and for being so open and honest, and willing to share his story for the purpose of being truly helpful to others. His sincerity in understanding that he doesn't have it all figured out, and is still learning, will help further him on the path to awakening. Aren't we all still learning? To assume we know what is best for ourselves and others, and to define things in our own way, stops us from listening to the Voice that can help lead us to the answer for the highest good of all concerned.

Children and Cyber-Bullying

There are more stories everyday about young children succumbing to suicide as a result of cyber-bullying, and bullying in general. What is cyber-bullying? Here is the definition from unicef.org's website: "Cyberbullying is bullying with the use of digital technologies. It can take place on social media, messaging platforms, gaming platforms and mobile phones. It is repeated behavior, aimed at scaring, angering or shaming those who are targeted."

If you have a child who is being bullied, and need further assistance, you can contact Child Helpline International at the following link, which provides wonderful information and resources for extra help: https://www.childhelplineinternational.org/

It is most important when help starts in the home, when a parent or caregiver notices abnormal behavior from the child, and offers help and support when needed. This is important whether you have a child who is the one bullying other children or if he/she is being bullied by someone else. Children are also calling out for love, and that is why the bullying occurs. They don't often know how to express their fears and concerns, and if they don't have a strong support system, and an outlet to express themselves, they project their fears onto their peers. This doesn't make the behavior okay, but it does require extra professional help sometimes, often with a school counselor or parent at home. If that doesn't work, seeking help from the website above or other professional sources is important. **In addition, it could be a very helpful thing to start teaching children not to identify with social platforms. In other words, they may use it, but teach them that it doesn't represent who they are in truth. They don't have to equate that platform with who they are as a beautiful Spirit. You may educate them on the idea that others may use it for purposes that hurt others, but it doesn't mean your child has to believe what they say...and it's never personal. If your child starts thinking like this from the start, it will help them not take it too seriously. It's worth a try.**

It is helpful for children to know from the moment they are born that they are loved and valued, and have a beautiful purpose in life. Parents can demonstrate this just by being unconditionally loving. It doesn't require specific words, but they will know you care for them by your demonstration. No one is perfect, and everyone makes mistakes, so if you feel you didn't start off on a "good" note with your child, please forgive yourself. Everyone does the best they can with the awareness they have at the time. Every moment is a new moment, and therefore you can start fresh with your child at any moment you choose. Also, you can create "safe" places where children can act out their frustrations while you monitor their behavior at the same time, so they are not hurting themselves or others. Teach them they are powerful enough to have what they need without manipulating others to get it. It's never too early to positively reinforce good behavior as well.

If a child is being bullied, after doing whatever you can to keep them safe and offer whatever support is needed, it may be helpful at some point to explain to the child that the person bullying them is also hurting and it is not personal, even if it seems scary. This doesn't mean they shouldn't tell someone. They should definitely be encouraged to tell someone what is happening to the best of their ability. This will teach the child healthier problem-solving techniques, so they learn they don't have to choose to project their own fears back onto the other person. This also goes for the child who is bullying. If there is a care giver involved that can help teach the child other ways of handling anger and fear, it is a good start. Obviously, in some cases it may still play out in a way that is violent where someone gets hurt. It's hard when parents don't feel they are in control of what happens. This is why doing the best you can, starting in the home, and then seeking other forms of help if you need it, is important. Also, children learn by positive reinforcement, not negative or punishing messages. It may seem like a child will respond positively to harsh punishment, but it will most likely get projected out on someone else later. A parent can use discipline and set boundaries, of course. If it comes from the right mind it will be helpful. **Ask the Holy Spirit to assist you in using the situation for its purposes, and trust that you will get the help you need.**

Here is an article I read recently on Bullycide, a term for suicide as a result of bullying:

According to Julie Cerel, president of the nonprofit American Association of Suicidology, bullycide is a misleading term. "Suicide is never caused by just one thing — lots of people are bullied who don't commit suicide," she tells Yahoo Lifestyle. "Pointing to one event oversimplifies a complicated issue and makes prevention more difficult."

Data published by the Centers for Disease Control and Prevention (CDC) supports that point. According to the CDC website, kids who are bullied — and those who bully — are at a higher risk for suicide. However, most kids who are involved in bullying don't attempt suicide.

Cerel says various factors can be at play, such as pathology (if a person has mental health issues, for example) or, in the case of younger people, impulsiveness. And per the CDC, kids at risk for suicide often deal with many types of stressors, including peer, romantic, family, and mental. "Bullying can be the last event that's reported on, but we often don't know the trajectory of what leads a person there," says Cerel.

Unfortunately, there's no one-size-fits-all checklist to help pinpoint if a person is contemplating suicide, whether or not the person is being bullied. "However, if a kid is clearly stating that they don't want to live, parents should open that conversation," says Cerel.

Being empathetic and lending an ear are also key. "Saying things like 'Things will get better' is often ineffective, since people who are suicidal experience cognitive constriction, a state of mind that prevents the belief that there's hope," says Cerel.

In the case of cyberbullying, parents should have meaningful conversations about what their kids are reading online. "It can be effective to do this before the teenage years, when kids still value the opinion of their parents over their peers," says Cerel. "Social media can be a teachable moment."

When anyone you know, whether a child or an adult is contemplating suicide, try to make sure someone is always with them, or keep calling them, not to lecture, just to be there for support. If they say they are okay, stay with them a while anyway, and encourage them to get help from a trained mental health professional to see if they are at risk for self-harm. As a parent in the home, if there is mental illness in the family, openly speak about it in a routine kind of way so children are trained to not feel ashamed to share their feelings and stories. Encourage their feelings without judging them, and make it known feelings serve a powerful purpose. Growing up in a household such as this will better prepare them as adults to answer honestly when someone asks them how they are doing.

When you notice friends or family members keeping their distance, and it is unusual for them to do so, stay on top of it. Call, text, or visit them often. You might say to them you've noticed they don't seem like themselves. Try not to pressure them into getting back to you, which may not help someone who is already depressed and who may feel guilty for not responding. Support them and remind them you are there for them, but again without the pressure for them to respond in the way you think they should. Just pay attention so they don't move too deep into a hopeless state.

I read about someone who was experiencing depression, who said, "One of the main reasons I didn't talk to people was my experience that people would try to dismiss or minimize my feelings out of love and an attempt to help. But it just made me feel inferior. Like, I should be able to 'just think of my family,' or 'don't let things get you down.' What would have helped? Just be with the person, watch movies and eat junk food. Convince them to go for walks. More than feeling like you have to say something, just be there for them. That is what they need."

If you have lost a child to suicide, please be kind to yourself. When you are ready, try practicing using some of the ideas in this chapter. Just as we can't control an adult's choice to take their life, we can't control a child's choice either. We can be guiding lights, and just do the best we can in their development. **Remember, behind every child is a wise soul who is also learning higher lessons that we can't see. How do we know what the best outcome is for anyone? All we can do is do our best to demonstrate what it means to be love, act from our right minds when necessary, and trust that the Holy Spirit is working with us. Everything will be okay.**

Additional Commentary on Suicide from the Perspective of A Course In Miracles

For anyone who is studying the Course, it is quite clear from the beginning that it's not saying the same thing as any other spiritual path. Its non-dualistic thought system gives rise to a completely different interpretation of the world, the purpose of our relationships within this world, and our personal lives in general. Since suicide is one of the forms that death can take in the world, and it is the focus of this chapter, I will comment on the Course's perspective of death, in which suicide is one form.

According to the Course, death is a thought in the mind, and has nothing to do with the body. If there is no world, as the Course says, there can be no body that is doing anything. It is the mind that believes in such things. **The ego itself originated from the insane illusion that death was accomplished in our attacking God so that we could be a separate, individual self, apart from God, which makes us "special." This ego idea is a murderous thought, and symbolizes the death of God, and is also the ultimate suicide attempt – the death of our true Self as Christ.** The projection of this insane belief had to follow as a result of guilt, and that is why the world and how we sometimes attempt to destroy our bodies within this world, is also insane and unreal.

As one reads the Course, it is clear that the Course's focus is on content and purpose, rather than form of any kind. The ego has a purpose for death, and no matter what the form is of our passing, its purpose is to prove that the separation is real. The unconscious fear that follows from that idea is that God is punishing us for our "sin" of leaving him by taking back the life we have stolen from Him. To repeat, we all know the common expression, "I am a God-fearing person." Although the intent of this statement is probably sincere, it is simply not true that God is to be feared. God is perfect love.

Once we learn to look at ourselves and the world with the Holy Spirit, it also encourages us to see death differently. We can see that death takes many forms, including suicide, but with the same content behind it, which is serving the ego's purpose by making us feel alone and separate in a cold, cruel world. Looking with the Holy Spirit helps us to inquire deeper into the nature of our assumptions, understanding that our perceptions are false because they are based on a faulty premise that we are the victims of our circumstances with no way out; trapped in world that doesn't love us. Afterall, the ego says, "I didn't make this world! That person is the problem, or the world is the problem." If we continue to think this way, there *is* no way out, which is how the ego wants it. The Holy Spirit is the answer to every problem we think we have because in choosing it, it reminds us that everything we have taught ourselves about the nature of reality has been wrong. It takes a humble Spirit to admit this. We've built our lives on believing we were right about most things, but in my opinion…thank God we were wrong!

From the Course's perspective, the ego has built a defense that says life in a body (which includes our birth and death) is real, and *that* defense is animated when one judges something like suicide to be more "special" than another form of death. In other words, the same thought system is behind all forms of death if it is serving the ego's purpose. The thought system of the ego is a mistake, and that includes the thought of suicide. It is an error, but not a sin. The error is that we want to keep the unconscious guilt alive in our minds, because that is how the ego says, "I'm alive." The mistaken thinking that we can be born is no different than the mistake in thinking we can really die. The whole game of the ego is to make the world the problem, and so we keep seeking outside ourselves for the answer that will make us happy. That answer will never be found outside, but only in our minds, where both the mistaken choice and the answer are found.

Suicide is less likely to be a choice when one learns that another, more gentle and loving experience can replace it. The Course makes the following striking statement about this other way in which we can experience our illusory passing, which occurs when we turn to the Holy Spirit and think like Him. It is this:

> *Yet there is a kind of death that has a different source. It does not come because of hurtful thoughts and raging anger at the universe. It merely signifies the end has come for usefulness of body function-ing. And so it is discarded as a choice, as one lays by a garment now outworn.*[21] *This is what death should be; a quiet choice, made joyfully and with a sense of peace, because the body has been kindly used to help the Son of God along the way he goes to God.*[22]

Furthermore, suicide is just one form in which the ego uses the body for the purpose of attack, since our belief in sin is what drives attack.

> *The central lesson is always this; that what you use the body for it will become to you. Use it for sin or for attack, which is the same as sin, and you will see it as sinful. Because it is sinful it is weak, and being weak, it suffers and dies. Use it to bring the word of God to those who have it not, and the body becomes holy. Because it is holy it cannot be sick, nor can it die. When its usefulness is done it is laid by, and that is all. The mind makes this decision, as it makes all decisions that are responsible for the body's condition.*[23]

The key here is that we don't want to make decisions on our own, but instead listen to God's Voice, which will tell us when we have fulfilled our role. We can then be at peace regardless if we stay or go.

Can Suicide Come From a Right-Minded Decision?

Someone once asked, "Is suicide ever made from a right-minded decision?" It's possible that in certain cases a suicide could be a reflection of that person being in their right mind *if*, for example, that person is faced with a terminal illness, and is experiencing excruciating pain, and therefore may choose suicide to release themselves from the intensity of the pain. If this is done without judgment or guilt, then it could be a right-minded decision. However, there may still be lessons to be learned in the mind, in which that person would reincarnate and perhaps work through any unresolved material. Purpose is behind everything, and when we recognize the purpose in all that we do, and continue to work on remembering that our Will is one with God's Will, which is that we don't have to suffer, then choices can be made with peace.

In general, suicide is not a solution, because in most cases the mental pain that one attempts to alleviate doesn't disappear just because the body is gone. The mind keeps on going after our seeming death.

We still have to work through our lessons. **So, why not use our lives as opportunities to forgive our grievances? We should never stop seeking the Truth until we find it. In doing this, we work through and eventually experience the joy and peace of God, which is what we are always seeking.**

Physician-Assisted Suicide

I mentioned in a statement above that sometimes suicide may be a reflection of a right-minded choice. There has been a controversy for a long time regarding physician-assisted suicide, and whether it is an appropriate practice. I would like to share with you an article on this that I read recently, and then I will comment on it.

> "*Physician-assisted suicide is a practice where an attending doctor has the legal authority to offer a lethal prescription medication to someone who is terminally ill. The patient must usually be in a state of suffering, and it is often required to make the request of their doctor more than once to have it become a solution.*
>
> *Most states in the U.S. prohibit a physician-assisted suicide, although Oregon, Washington, Vermont, California, and Colorado have all legalized the practice if a specific set of steps are followed. Hawaii joined this group of states in 2019. Even though it is considered illegal, The Hastings Center notes that empirical studies have shown the act of PAD (physician-assisted death) to be an underground practice that is not actively prosecuted if it is not actively discussed.*
>
> *Alternatives to a lethal prescription include sedation to keep someone unconscious until their bodies cease to work because of their terminal illness. Some patients even decide to voluntarily stop eating and drinking to prevent their end-of-life suffering.*
>
> *Because we should be offering people with a terminal illness the state-of-the-art palliative care they deserve, the pros and cons of legalizing physician-assisted suicide in the United States and around the world deserve some consideration.*"

List of the Pros of Legalizing Physician-Assisted Suicide (from the same article)

1. ***The right to die should be a matter of choice instead of legislation.***
    We can choose numerous aspects of life without government interfer-ence, but the right to die is not generally one of them. Whether it is due to societal stigma or a religious view of suicide that is unfavorable, those with a terminal illness lose the ability to stop their own suffering. People should have the choice to dictate what happens to them. Some people want to live as long as *they possibly can, but if a severe medical condition makes that life unbearable, there should be options which allow it as well.*

2. ***It is used as a last resort option in all cases.***
    Many doctors favor the legalization of physician-assisted suicide for those who are already dying on the condition that their suffering can-not find relief in any other way. It is much more humane than the alternatives which some people might choose to avoid a protracted death.

    Dr. Marcia Angell was one of the first 14 petitioners in Massa-chusetts to place the Death with Dignity Act on the ballot. Her father decided to kill himself with a firearm rather than endure metastatic cancer of the prostate because of the laws concerning death. PAD would allow healers to continue to do their job as well as possible, with the understanding that their actions would help to bring peace.

3. ***There are specific legal requirements that must be met first.***
    In Washington State, the Death with Dignity Act requires a patient to be terminally ill with less than six months to live according to the diagnosis from their doctor. Only qualified patients can make a writ-ten request for medication that they must self-administer to end their life. If an adult patient is not competent because of a mental illness or altered state, then it would still be illegal to offer a lethal prescription – even if the written request was offered.

    If the competency of the patient is established, then there must also be two witnesses who sign the request as well. The witnesses cannot be a relative, someone entitled to a portion of their estate, or an individual employed by the facility where the patient is receiving care.

4. ***Doctors take a minimal role in the physician-assisted suicide process.***

   When Americans think about the issue of PAD, the name that comes to mind for them is Dr. Jack Kevorkian. This man would become infamous because of his strange proposals and unorthodox experiments, earning the nickname of "Dr. Death." Kevorkian would voluntarily help people to take their lives, although 60% of them were not terminally ill. He would eventually spend time in prison for his activities.

   The reality of legalizing physician-assisted suicide is that doctors play a minimal role in this process. In the State of Oregon, there were only 374 physicians participating in the Death with Dignity Act program, representing 0.6% of the state's total doctors. 62% of them had only written one lethal prescription without any knowledge of who had decided to take the medication or not.

5. ***It allows a patient to have control over their final decisions.***

   When a terminal illness is present, then the quality of life for the individual can drop severely and rapidly. It can also be an exceptionally painful experience. Even if medication can help to control the discomfort that they experience, the drugs can change how an individual interacts with their loved ones. If the disease takes a prolonged time to finally cause the physical body to succumb, the toll it takes on the physical, emotional, and financial health of the family can be significant. Legalizing physician-assisted suicide can help to provide relief for everyone in this situation while preserving the dignity of the patient.

6. ***There is no longer any burden of guilt experienced by the patient.***

   When someone receives a diagnosis which is terminal, there can be an element of shock at first. It can be challenging to come to grips with the idea that one only has six months or less to live. Then the emotional reaction occurs, which often includes guilt because the patient feels like the care that they require to stay alive provides a tremendous burden on their family. By legalizing physician-assisted suicide, the hardships of this transitory time for everyone can be reduced because the patient is taking control over their circumstances.

7. ***The outcome is typically the same, no matter what the process is***

at the end of the day.

When there is a debate about the pros and cons of legalizing physician-assisted suicide, the different key points usually involve the process that is "ethical" or "moral" for someone to have their life end. The reality for patients in this situation is that they are already facing an end-of-life scenario. Even if they decide against a PAD, there is still an excellent chance that death will be coming for them soon. The family will still be grieving for that person. Shouldn't it be left to those involved to make the choice instead of an oversight committee or government?"

In my personal opinion, when one is in a situation as described above, where the diagnosis of "terminal illness" is stated, and the patient is in extreme pain, it can be considered an act of kindness to allow that individual to make the very personal choice of ending their life with assistance from a professional physician. However, if one is not experiencing a terminal illness, and is unhappy with their life, and looking for an escape from problems, this raises another issue. In other words, the person might not realize that they wouldn't really be escaping their problems by ending their life. They would just have to come back (reincarnate) and continue to learn their lessons, and may even experience the same types of problems until all is forgiven and released. So we don't escape our problems by death. The Course teaches that we escape problems by forgiving the guilt that is associated with our problems, which leads to *life*.

None of us are ever in a position to judge what is best for someone else, nor what the best outcome is for everyone involved, because we can't see the bigger picture. Therefore, the practical thing is to try to help the suicidal person consider a change of mind. It may be helpful to remember that no one really "dies." As mentioned above, death is a thought in the mind, or more accurately, a belief. When the mind no longer chooses to dream of a world of birth and death (the idea of separation) the world will simply disappear. As long as we see a world at all, it only means we wish to see it. There is still something we think it is bringing us. As long as we do see it, we can choose *how* we experience this world. We can use it for the Holy Spirit's purpose of forgiveness, or the ego's purpose of maintaining the illusion of separation.

The Course explains that the guilt over the separation was so terrible, we find all kinds of ways to "kill" ourselves so that we can say, "I am unworthy of God's love, and I have punished myself so God won't punish me." **Remember…God doesn't know His Son as anything He is not. God only knows His Son as whole, perfect, and innocent. And you are His Son. So, if you are entertaining thoughts that aren't loving, please recognize that this is your choice, but not God's. God doesn't have anything to do with it. He just wants you to return to Wholeness, but to return to Him in Joy, not fear or sadness.** This can be done through forgiving the things in your life that upset you, and forgiving yourself for dreaming them up in the first place. You are not your dream, but you are the dreamer of your dream, and you can change your mind about it. This is true power!

One final word to those that may be struggling with the death of a loved one through suicide, or by any other means: Be gentle and patient with yourself and allow yourself to grieve if you need to. You are not responsible for another's choices, but only for your own. At some point, you may wish to remember that you can never really lose anyone, because all minds are joined. You and your loved ones will be reunited in Spirit, and it will be a celebration! Your loved ones in Spirit appreciate you remembering the loving things they did and the loving thoughts that were shared, seeing them as whole and innocent. In reality, we are all still at home in God, because nothing happened to change that reality. We are experiencing a dream of separation, but we are awakening from the dream "together." When we are awake, we will simply know that we are ONE, and have never left God, and that nothing happened to change that reality.

In summary, one of the most helpful tools we can use, whether it's for ourselves or others, is the idea that we can pay attention to that whisper before it becomes a roar; to see the signs for calls for help in ourselves and others before it can escalate. That is at least a starting point. It's better to side on being cautious about a loved one's unusual behavior than just assuming everything is okay. Suicide doesn't discriminate. Remember that every second human beings can change, and can choose to hold a different perception. You are worth the consistent effort to live out your life with integrity, peace, and joy.

Please Note: In the US, for extra help, people can call the National Suicide Prevention Lifeline: 800-273-8255

Page for Personal Notes

CHAPTER 5

FLIP YOUR SCRIPT

It is the Holy Spirit's goal to help us escape from the dream world by teaching us how to reverse our thinking and unlearn our mistakes. Forgiveness is the Holy Spirit's great learning aid in bringing this thought reversal about.[1]

When I was thinking about this chapter, and trying to think of an example to use in regard to changing my mind about a particular person from the ego's interpretation to the Holy Spirit's (flipping my script), I realized that, currently, I don't have anyone in my life whom I have not forgiven. This is because I have learned not to judge people for their behavior. It doesn't mean I agree with certain people and their behaviors, but I don't judge them. Jesus didn't always agree with people's behavior, but he didn't judge it. He wouldn't make it real. Judging a dream figure or the dream itself does make the dream real. The whole point of the Course is recognizing that there is no world of time and space, only an illusory projection of it. The world we see is in our minds. If we react to the world with our egos, we are reinforcing the dream. When we respond with the Holy Spirit, we are undoing the belief in dreams. So, we can act on things, but we can do it with our internal teacher, the Holy Spirit, which leads us to peace.

I don't believe in enemies, so I have never really had any enemies. But I did have to work on forgiving people in my dream script that pushed my buttons, even if I had never met them. I know it is difficult sometimes to forgive those who we feel are doing great injustices to other people. For example, all the stories we hear on the news about African Americans being abused by those police officers who use

105

unnecessary force can easily push my buttons if I forget to forgive it. In no way (at this level), is it loving to allow that to happen. But at some point, as a Course student, it's helpful to recognize that holding onto grievances hurts us, even though it feels like we are justified in holding onto them. It doesn't mean we don't take action if necessary, but it can be done without violence.

Martin Luther King, Jr. was a powerful example of one who listened to the Holy Spirit. He took action, but it was inspired action. He also believed that hate breeds more hate, and we need to answer hate with love. Here is a quote from him about forgiveness:

"We must develop and maintain the capacity to forgive. He who is devoid of the power to forgive is devoid of the power to love."

Forgiveness in this world is love in action. If we don't forgive, we are cutting off love within ourselves. Forgiveness doesn't mean you have to spend time with or hang out with the people you are forgiving if you don't want to. It's not about behavior. Forgiveness means you are no longer a prisoner of your own or someone else's hate. You are free.

Stories of Rodney King and George Floyd - Lessons in Forgiveness

As I write this (May 30, 2020) there are violent protests breaking out all over the United States, including where I live in Los Angeles, over the passing of an African American man named George Floyd at the hands of a white police officer. Police cars are burning, and stores are being looted; consequently, there was a curfew just placed all over Los Angeles to allow for order, cleanup, and safety. This is a story that is currently developing, so I may have updates later, putting it within the context of the Course's message. I can hear helicopters constantly circling our area and police sirens that have been re-occurring for the last several hours. There is a protest scheduled this evening right around the corner from where we live. The acts of violence remind me of the Rodney King situation and the Los Angeles riots back in 1992, and I think this story deserves another review. If anyone reading this isn't aware of what happened, here is an explanation by Wikipedia:

*The 1992 Los Angeles riots were a series of riots and civil distur-
bances that occurred in Los Angeles County in April and May
1992. Unrest began in South Central Los Angeles on April 29,
after a trial jury acquitted four officers of the Los Angeles Police
Department (LAPD) for usage of excessive force in the arrest and
beating of Rodney King, which had been videotaped and widely
viewed in TV broadcasts.*

*The rioting spread throughout the Los Angeles metropolitan
area, as thousands of people rioted over a six-day period following the announcement of the verdict. Widespread looting, assault,
arson, and murder occurred during the riots, which local police
could not control due to lack of personnel and resources against the
sheer number of rioters. The complete disorder in the Los Angeles
area was only resolved after the California Army National Guard,
the United States military, and several federal law enforcement
agencies intervened.*

*By the time the riots ended, 63 people had been killed, 2,383
people had been injured, more than 12,000 had been arrested, and
estimates of property damage were over $1 billion, much of which
disproportionately affected Koreatown, Los Angeles. LAPD Chief
of Police Daryl Gates, who had already announced his resignation
by the time of the riots, was attributed with much of the blame.*

I'll never forget one night during that time when a curfew was
placed in Los Angeles from 6pm to the next morning. I was at my
boyfriend's house at the time, and I wanted to get home fast. It was just
before 6pm, and my boyfriend wanted me to stay over, but I insisted
on leaving because I didn't want to stay over that night. He gave me
a knife to take with me in the car, just in case. What?!! It was the
strangest feeling having him give me a knife, which didn't ease my
tension. There were stories of people coming up to cars and bashing in
the windows, beating anyone they could find; scary stuff in the dream
world. I started driving home and it was the strangest feeling…I was
practically the only car on the road, driving down Wilshire Blvd., one
of the busiest and most famous streets in the world. Here I was, driving

along at a very high speed down Wilshire, with hardly any cars in sight. It was like a twilight zone episode. It was also eerily quiet. Thankfully, I made it home just a little after the curfew time. At this time I wasn't practicing the Course, so I just trusted that I would be safe. It was a strange time, but an important one. It was a lesson for all of us to bring attention to abusive behavior, but also to learn to forgive, for those able to use it for that purpose.

At the level of the world, the way George Floyd passed (along with other African Americans at the hands of overly abusive police officers) is clearly an injustice, and it is appropriate to speak up about it, but this is also a lesson in forgiveness. **Remember, all injustice, when viewed with true Vision, is a call for love and union.** I will speak more about this below.

The Course wouldn't be against stopping harm or bringing an event to trial when one appears to be harming another. The Course's perspective in a situation like this would be to remember to be normal, and do whatever you think is appropriate, but it can be done from your right-mind, without violence. Think of Gandhi's remarkable example of freeing India from colonial rule with no violence. Furthermore, there is nothing holy about using violence to stop violence. There *is* holiness, however, in allowing yourself to be used as a vessel for positive change when you are using it for the Holy Spirit's purpose. For it to be lasting change, it starts from within one's own mind. Violence may bring an *illusory* change, but it's only temporary until each mind starts recognizing that the world won't change until the people of the world have inner change by choosing peace.

When you attempt to change the effect (the world) without dealing with its cause (the unconscious guilt in the mind that gets projected out), the cause of guilt will remain, and with it, its effects. If we look at a situation such as the George Floyd tragedy with the right mind, we can see that all violence, no matter what form it takes, is a call for love as I've mentioned before several times. We are one with all our brothers and sisters, and when we attack others, we attack ourselves. Again, there is nothing wrong with protesting or voicing an opinion, nor bringing people to justice in regard to stopping harmful behavior, which is often necessary. It's our attitude and state of mind that matters; *how and with whom* we take these actions.

It's easy to become distracted by the ego, and get sucked into its thought system, so that we drown out the Voice of the Holy Spirit. When this happens, we are shutting out another curriculum, the Atonement. We can't choose it as long as we are listening to two teachers simultaneously that represent completely opposing views, finding ourselves going back and forth. This results *not* in change, but confusion. Until this is recognized, the mind will continue to be split between illusions and truth, so that your reality will remain obscure to you.

The distractions of the ego may seem to interfere with your learning, but the ego has no power to distract you unless you give it the power to do so. The ego's voice is an hallucination. You cannot expect it to say, "I am not real." Yet you are not asked to dispel your hallucinations alone. You are merely asked to evaluate them in terms of their results to you. If you do not want them on the basis of loss of peace, they will be removed from your mind for you.[2]

Every response to the ego is a call to war, and war does deprive you of peace. Yet in this war there is no opponent. This is the reinterpretation of reality that you must make to secure peace, and the only one you need ever make.[3]

These statements are reminding us that in truth there is only one mind. All of us are one Son of God. So, when we are attacking others, we are attacking ourselves. This is why there really isn't an opponent. The war is always against the self for believing it attacked God. Fortunately, no matter how much we believe in this, reality hasn't changed and never will. God just wants us to wake up and return to Him in peace.

A while back I read the following quote from an anonymous source, which really drove the point home to me about holding onto grievances: "Hatred corrodes the container it's carried in." The Course says the same thing in a different way, but when I heard it stated this way, it somehow inspired me to search my mind more and let go of any judgmental thoughts about myself or others. I continually asked myself, "Why would I want to hurt myself?" Since all minds are joined, if I am thinking about another person with hatred, I am really saying "I hate myself." I can also choose to remember that people can call out for love in vicious ways, but nonetheless, they are still calling for love. When we hold onto judgments we hurt ourselves, period. Fear and judgment are probably the two most imbalanced ideas we can hold onto, which lowers our vibrations and manifests as sickness, ultimately the result of the belief in separation. The irony is that even though fear is a judgment, we do need to let go of the judgment of fear, by forgiving ourselves when we feel it.

So, I will use the situations above as an example of how I flipped my script from the ego's script to the Holy Spirit's script. That's what this chapter is about, and what the chapter title means. The ego's script is the world of time and space, which includes all the different dimensions of time. It was all projected out at the same time as a defense against the truth of our oneness with God. The Holy Spirit's script is looking at the ego's script with forgiveness instead of judgment. When we are flipping the script, we are choosing to make the shift from the ego's perspective to the Holy Spirit's perspective. We aren't changing the actual script, the events in the dream. An example would be that if the planet earth is our chosen illusory home during this lifetime (as opposed to other planets or star systems) then when we are forgiving the ego's script, it is possible to switch dimensions of time so that we might experience a different version of earth, since there are many parallel versions of earth itself. We might still see the same people, and certain events might still play out, but we would *experience* them differently, with peace instead of conflict. There could be a war going on, but you might experience the war without any conflict because your mind has become free of conflict.

Remember, the Course says that the miracle saves us time, because when we choose it, we are playing leap frog, basically skipping over parts of our script, which means time is collapsing for us. Certain lessons have been learned so we might switch to a different part of the script where a gentler scenario plays out. This is the beauty of this path! When you do your forgiveness work, results are happening even if you don't see it with your body's eyes. I encourage you to keep it up and treat it like a game you are playing! It really is a choice that we make as to whether we are making the game serious or remembering to laugh, simply *because* it is a game.

So, how did I flip my script using the examples above? I realized that my "sad" feelings about the two men's stories mentioned above and what played out was the ego's script. I remembered that I was mentally reviewing this script, and that I wasn't really here. I recognized that I was feeling sad because I was making the ego's script real, and that I chose to feel sad in my mind first, and then projected that sadness outside of myself onto this situation, so that the guilt was in the perpetrators, not in me. That's where my ego wanted it. **I was judging illusions, trying to figure out how one illusion could be substituted for a better one, rather than choosing the judgment of the Holy Spirit over the ego's judgment, the only "real" choice/judgment there is. Choosing to see innocence or the non-judgmental perspective of the Holy Spirit is a correction for the ego's judgment of sin, guilt, and fear.**

I was starting to "flip my script" by being aware of my part in interpreting the situation with the ego. I then forgave myself and my projections of guilt onto the seeming perpetrators, so that I could become an observer of the event without judgment or blame, and free both myself and whoever else was involved. I made up the ego's script so I could make the world the problem. Peace returned the instant I remembered not to judge it. I also remembered that I don't know what lessons are being learned by all parties involved, and that events playing out have a purpose. This process can be used with any situation or person.

Also, the following forgiveness exercise offered by Pursah in Gary's book, *The Disappearance of the Universe*, can be applied to any person, situation, or event that disturbs your peace. She says, "*As you practice this kind of forgiveness, the Holy Spirit will do its part in removing the unconscious guilt from your mind, and perform His healing of the universe.*" Remember, this is also expressing what it means to be in a non-dualistic state of mind. Here is the exercise, that is, the thoughts to direct at those who have disturbed your peace:

> *You're not really there. If I think you are guilty or the cause of the problem, and if I made you up, then the imagined guilt and fear*

must be in me. Since the separation from God never occurred, I forgive "both" of us for what we haven't really done. Now there is only innocence, and I join with the Holy Spirit in peace.[4]

Once you forgive something, it doesn't mean you can't be helpful in form in some way if that is what you are guided to do. That can be a reflection of love, too. When you return your mind to peace, you are being truly helpful to the Sonship, and that love can take the form of some kind of action, but not always. It doesn't have to. For me, in this particular situation, doing my forgiveness work was being truly helpful, because all minds are joined, and as I forgive, the whole mind benefits. Notice how I didn't need to try and change the script or the event in some way, but only change my mind by switching to a different interpretation of it. I was guided to write about this, which is an inspired action that I felt good about taking, for the purposes of using it for forgiveness.

Further, when you need to forgive something, you can use whatever right-minded ideas are helpful in the Course that inspires you to stay on track. Everyone has their "go to" lines in the Course that work for them. I have mine, too. I have noticed that when I actually do the forgiveness work, it really helps return my mind to a state of peace. This means *practicing* the steps we are taught in the Course.

Jesus talks a lot in the Course about what we invest our faith in for salvation. Until we learn to change our minds, most of us will keep trying to find salvation outside of ourselves, in people, substances, and relationships in general. The following powerful section in the Course always keeps me on track when I am tempted to seek salvation outside myself, or blame someone or something else for my upset:

The secret of salvation is but this: That you are doing this unto yourself. No matter what the form of the attack, this still is true. Whoever takes the role of enemy and of attacker, still is this the truth. Whatever seems to be the cause of any pain and suffering you feel, this is still true. For you would not react at all to figures in a dream you knew that you were dreaming. Let them be as hateful and as vicious as they may, they could have no effect on you unless you failed to recognize it is your dream.[5]

Jesus goes on to explain that when we accept this idea into our minds, it will free us from suffering, no matter what form the suffering takes. This is the only lesson we need to learn to be free. So, why don't we accept it? The guilt is very strong. Anytime we are attempting to forgive, it is always for the purpose of removing guilt from our minds, the ultimate block to the awareness of love's presence. Thinking with the ego is a habit, and habits can be changed. A habit is changed when we first decide that we *want* to change. The desire has to be there. When we make the decision first, the steps to get there will follow, but it often takes a step by step, thought by thought process to allow the change to occur. The mind needs to be trained to think differently. When you want to build muscle in the body, you train for it by building yourself up with practice and exercise daily. With the mind, you build the muscle of your mind by practicing right-minded thoughts of forgiveness daily with whatever comes up that disturbs your peace. **It takes discipline and abundant willingness to form a new habit. We can never really lack discipline and motivation because we were all motivated to choose the ego. So, it's just a matter of re-focusing your motivation so that it is directed toward your spiritual awakening**.

Coming back to depression for a moment, if you are experiencing a deep depression and you feel you aren't motivated to make an internal shift yet, ask yourself whether it's really a matter of motivation as you remind yourself of the statement above. We are always motivated, so it's a matter of where we are putting that motivation. Then, ask yourself what the very next step is that you can take in that moment. What is the next loving thought you can hold, even if that means you stay with that thought a while. If it's an action that you take, what is the very next, simplest step that helps you to move around a bit. Maybe it's taking a shower, or going to your computer to write an email, or whatever it is that keeps you moving. It's all about a step-by-step process. If you take a shower, and that's all you can muster up in that moment, practice being okay with that, and not judging it. You can also be okay with doing nothing, without judging yourself. Even doing nothing is something. Keep taking things in small doses. Walking outside in the sunshine for even just a few minutes can really help lift one's mood. If one idea seems more exciting than another, follow the one that is most exciting first. **The whole point is that whatever you do, practice non-judgment with yourself.**

I have found that having an attitude of gratitude also cultivates an experience of abundance. In other words, the abundance I feel has nothing to do with getting things in the world. God created me in love, in His likeness, which is everything I could possibly want or need. When I think this way, I can trust that whatever worldly needs I may have will take care of themselves, because I have sought the Kingdom of Heaven first. It feels really good to let go of outcomes and expectations of how the world should look, or how people should act. From all my experience in practicing the Course, I have learned that when I just focus on my state of mind, and do the best I can to be in my right mind no matter what is going on, then the effect will take care of itself. It takes practice to trust this process. The more you practice, the more the benefits will be apparent.

The Practice of Flipping Your Script on a Daily Basis

Part of the work of the Course, and what helps us to "flip our scripts," is sorting out the false from the true. This means that on a daily basis, you practice recognizing the thoughts you are thinking with the ego, that is, when you are misperceiving. When your peace is disturbed, that means there is a perception you are holding that is not representative of the truth as it is in reality. Ask yourself if this is what you really want to feel, and then remind yourself that you can look at it differently. This helps train your mind to remember that it is always choosing. This process works better if you remember to put the Holy Spirit in charge of your day, right after you get up in the morning. I always ask the Holy Spirit to be in charge of my decision-making. This means that I trust I will remember to choose the Holy Spirit's interpretation of anything that comes up during the day that challenges my peace.

The beginning of my day — you might start with something different — starts with the following statement: *Holy Spirit, please help me to choose the joy of God instead of pain today. I want to experience peace above all else. Please use my body for your purposes, so that I can be truly helpful.* Then, I let it go and start my day. If nothing comes up during the day that disturbs my peace, I just accept the beauty of that and celebrate with gratitude. If something does come up, I remind myself that I must have been thinking with the ego, or else I wouldn't feel that way. Or maybe there was a judgment I was holding, which means I forgot to put the Holy Spirit in charge of my thoughts. If it's hard for me to change my mind, I just remind myself that I am choosing to feel this way right now, and when I am ready I will change my mind, but I remain open to learning, not assuming I'm right in my perception. Perhaps I've been wrong in my thinking. This opens up my mind to the idea that there is another way of looking at things, and what do I have to lose by asking? This is a meaningful question to ask, because it directs the mind to a right-minded perspective.

The ideas above are inspired by the section that I love in the Course called *Rules for Decision* in Chapter 30, *Section I.*[6] I recommend this section for review whenever you need a refresher of how you can work your way up to remembering that peace is what you really want, regardless of what the ego tells you; helping you "flip your script!" In my first book, *A Course in Health and Well-Being*, I also go over these steps in more detail.

So many people ask me how I apply the Course in my everyday life. It's been a process over time, and I want to encourage you that when you trust the process and stick with it, it is very helpful and beneficial in ways you might not see at first. I just follow the steps of forgiveness we are given in the Course to reverse our thinking and unlearn our mistakes, which is also what the Workbook helps us do. I also remind myself daily that I am dreaming. I practice noticing if my peace is disturbed so that I can correct my thoughts to reflect the Holy Spirit's perception.

The Workbook of the Course is the practical guide we are given, 365 lessons, to start the process of undoing the ego; learning how to undo the way we see now, so that we can learn to see with correct perception, which has nothing to do with the body's eyes, but how we are thinking about things. If the Course is your chosen path, and you haven't done the Workbook yet, I highly recommend you do it at some point. After you have done it once, you don't have to do it again unless you want to, or are guided to. The only rule in the Workbook is that you don't do more than one lesson in a day. It's okay to stay on one particular lesson for more than a day as most people do. No one really does the Workbook perfectly, but it doesn't mean you can't try! If you start the Workbook and are doing the lessons for a while, you might decide to take a break. When you start up again, it isn't necessary to go back to the beginning and start over unless you want to. You can just continue where you left off. There is no rule about that. We get a lot of questions about this. Simply follow the instructions in the introduction to the Workbook.

Another question we get is: "If I am a new student of the Course, where should I begin, with the text or workbook or both?" Again, there is no rule about what part of the Course you should begin with. For the sake of making the principles easier to understand, I always recommend that people start by reading the Manual for Teachers and Clarification of Terms sections. These sections explain the basic principles of the Course and gives Jesus's meanings and definitions of the terms He is using. Some of the definitions we are used to hearing in traditional Christianity are re-defined by Jesus to mean something different. So, if you start reading the text without any background of what the terms mean, it might be more difficult to follow. So, this is just a suggestion. It will become clear to you that Jesus is teaching something quite different from traditional Christianity, and he didn't start a religion. The basic principles of Christianity were based on the writings of the Apostle Paul. Jesus was teaching 2000 years ago what He is teaching in the Course today; pure-non-dualism. If you'd like a refresher on pure-non-dualism, I recommend you re-read Chapter 1 in this book and the Preface of the Course.

In order to accomplish the goal of the Course, the attainment of true peace, the "flipping of the script," from the ego's purpose to the

Holy Spirit's is necessary. I want to reiterate that forgiveness is what brings about this thought reversal. I am repeating this on purpose. There are other ideas that are necessary to accept before we can fully integrate them into our lives. For example, Jesus says, *There is nothing outside you. That is what you must ultimately learn, for it is the realization that the Kingdom of Heaven is restored to you.*[7] Also, *Heaven is not a place nor a condition. It is merely an awareness of perfect oneness, and the knowledge that there is nothing else; nothing outside this oneness, and nothing else within.*[8] This is clearly stating that if there is nothing outside this oneness, we must have made up everything else.

This is why the Course describes this world as a dream, because it doesn't represent perfect oneness. The fact that this can be a violent world, where one can harm another, or even the wish to attempt to harm another, can only mean that fear is the ruler here until we change our minds about what we are. There is no question that bodies can be destroyed, but we aren't our bodies; we are minds, which can't be destroyed. We are eternal beings. When we pass on from this life, the mind keeps on going, still dreaming of birth and death, until each one accepts the Atonement for himself, which is remembering we haven't left God, and we are always ONE with Him. It is fashionable to be as God created you. The ego is simply a fad that is going out of style.

This concept of "flipping our scripts" is only meaningful at the level of the world where we believe we are. It has no meaning in Heaven, because in Heaven there is nothing that opposes perfect oneness. We simply made a mistake in substituting illusion for truth; separation for wholeness. This was an error that just needs correction.

Perhaps a little review from the Course in how the substitution of illusion for truth produced the effect of separation would be helpful in motivating us to "flip our scripts" to the Holy Spirit's interpretation. Here it is, from the words of the Master, Jesus:

You who believe that God is fear made but one substitution. It has taken many forms, because it was the substitution of illusion for truth; of fragmentation for wholeness. It has become so splintered and subdivided and divided again, over and over, that it is now almost impossible to perceive it once was one, and still is what it was. That one error, which brought truth to illusion, infinity to time, and life to death, was all you ever made. Your whole world rests upon it. Everything you see reflects it, and every special relationship that you have ever made is part of it.[9]

*You may be surprised to hear how very different is reality from what you see. You do not realize the magnitude of that one error. It was so vast and so completely incredible that from it a world of total unreality **had** to emerge. What else could come of it? Its fragmented aspects are fearful enough, as you begin to look at them. But nothing you have seen begins to show you the enormity of the original error, which seemed to cast you out of Heaven, to shatter knowledge into meaningless bits of disunited perceptions, and to force you to make further substitutions.*[10]

*That was the first projection of error outward. The world arose to hide it, and became the screen on which it was projected and drawn between you and the truth. For truth extends inward, where the idea of loss is meaningless and only increase is conceivable. Do you really think it strange that a world in which everything is backwards and upside down arose from this projection of error? It was inevitable. For truth brought to this could only remain within in quiet, and take no part in all the mad projection by which this world was made. Call it not sin but madness, for such it was and so it still remains. Invest it not with guilt, for guilt implies it was accomplished in reality. And above all, **be not afraid of it**.*[11]

*When you seem to see some twisted form of the original error rising to frighten you, say only, **God is not fear, but Love**, and it will disappear. The truth will save you. It has not left you, to go out into the mad world and so depart from you. Inward is sanity; insanity is outside you.*[12]

As I reviewed these statements by Jesus, I had a rush of energy move through my entire being, which for me confirms the truth. He is explaining here the purpose of the world according to the ego! The world was made to hide the face of God, so we would forget where we came from, all because we believe we sinned by choosing to separate from His love. All we need to do is look at the world honestly, and all our projections of hatred and anger, judgment and blame, violence and death, and see what we have made. We can then ask ourselves, "Do we want this?"

When we start to realize that the world doesn't even come close to the love of God, then our awakening *from* the dream of separation will be the *only* thing that matters to us. This means that we live our lives, but with the Holy Spirit guiding us instead of the ego, understanding as we learn our lessons of forgiveness that we are furthering our progress in awakening from the dream. So we still need to do our part and learn that we can have a happy dream before God takes the final step and we return to the home we never left. As long as there is guilt in the mind, we keep coming back here until we forgive it all. There is no punishment or anyone keeping score. Afterall, we are eternal beings! There is no need to rush ourselves, but allow our process (the undoing of the ego to unfold naturally) and it will be done in Divine timing!

The Holy Spirit corrects our perceptions so we can see with true vision or Christ vision. This idea can be applied to anything that disturbs your peace, especially in the case where it seems there is an injustice done to yourself or someone else. Christ vision means that we are seeing things from another point of view, reflecting the thought system of the Holy Spirit, which helps us return to God and His knowledge. When we are seeing with Christ vision, we look at injustices differently, so instead of seeing attack, they become calls for love; or calls to join. If we see others suffering taking the form of attacking others, or some form of sickness, we would know that these are misperceptions, and so we would respond with gentleness and love. Since we wouldn't see it as an attack, there would be no need to defend. We are all calling for love in various ways, so when we see other's calling for it, we can recognize it is our own call as well. This makes us the same because we all share the same mind; which means we all share the part of the mind that is projecting the ego, or extending the Holy Spirit, and then the decision-maker that chooses between the two. This is why we are the same.

If challenges are looked at from a spiritual context such as this, it is much easier to forgive because we would understand that to condemn another would mean we are condemning ourselves. If we knew we were projecting, which is hurting ourselves, we wouldn't do it. So the key is catching ourselves when we notice we have slipped into egoic thinking. One way to know if we are choosing the Holy Spirit's perception or the ego's is how we treat other people and ourselves. You can tell a lot about someone by how they treat others. We can't give what we don't believe we have. The more the ego is undone, the more love reveals itself, and you will find it was always there, just hidden. The less guilt in the mind, the less suffering, period. The choices you make will reflect the love in your mind, completely aligning with your true Self. I have noticed this in my own life. As a result of practicing forgiveness for many years, I am in my "right mind" more often, and so the choices I make in my personal life reflect that state of mind, leading to a much more pleasant experience of what could have been an unpleasant one if I hadn't been practicing forgiveness. This is a great benefit of being in the business of forgiveness! The world and people don't have to change in order for you to experience peace, but when *you* change your mind *about* the world, this brings lasting peace to your mind. Whatever you do, then, would reflect peace. **This is what it means to say that it doesn't really matter *what* happens in the world, since the script is already written (and all of the dimensions of time within the script) but it does matter how you *think* about what happens, or what you *do* with what happens.** This is blasphemy to the ego that wants to convince you that the world in and of itself is important. That's because the ego made up the world of separation and wants to keep it the way it made it. God didn't make the world, because God is not insane. God is perfect love, and that perfect love remains intact regardless of the nightmare dreams we have made. **Our reality is abstract love; the world of perception is the world of dreams, and therefore cannot exist. This is the absolute Truth: God is.**

I mentioned that I may have updates on the current situation with the protests. Well, today is the 8th day of protests, which have now expanded across the globe. People from lots of other countries are standing together in support of police reform. The protests, at least for the time being, have become more peaceful. Even some officers are kneeling down with the protesters in support of the cause. In my opinion, this is people's way of joining, and whatever works to bring about a sense of connectedness with others is a good step. Although the Course says that only minds can join, and bodies do not really join (since we are not bodies) it is a helpful start for people to find ways of connecting with one another, and doing it peacefully. As a Course student, it is helpful for me to remember that we share *one* mind. My way of joining, then, would be to remember that *all* people are Spirit, whole and innocent in truth, and while I appear to be here in the world, I remember that *all* people are either calling for love or expressing love, and my response is always love, whatever form that takes.

In really tough times, it may be helpful to remember the following passages in the Workbook lesson, *All things are lessons God would have me learn*:[13]

> *This is the lesson God would have you learn: There is a way to look on everything that lets it be to you another step to Him, and to salvation of the world. To all that speaks of terror, answer thus: I will forgive, and this will disappear.*[14]
>
> *To every apprehension, every care and every form of suffering, repeat these selfsame words. And then you hold the key that opens Heaven's gate, and brings the Love of God the Father down to earth at last, to raise it up to Heaven. God will take this final step Himself. Do not deny the little steps He asks you take to Him.*[15]

The little steps He asks you to take are the steps of forgiveness by recognizing the Holy Spirit in all your brothers. Can this be hard for anyone who wants peace? If we truly want it, we will demonstrate that by our forgiveness.

It is very empowering to remember that when we don't feel peaceful, we are choosing to feel that way. From the moment we are born, we are taught to think that peace only happens when things in our lives go well. The Course is teaching us that regardless if things go well or not, we can still choose peace. Peace is a state of mind having nothing to do with the world. How is that for a "flip your script" moment? What is going on in the world is completely irrelevant to your peace. These are ideas that I remind myself of when I don't feel peaceful. It brings me back to remembering that my salvation lies *not* in the world, but in my own mind, because I get to choose my thoughts. **Remember, the ego and Holy Spirit represent mutually exclusive thought systems. One leads to peace, the other to conflict**.

During these times of social and political change, it is quite apparent that it is bringing to the surface deeply buried guilt over the separation from God, taking the form of civil unrest. We all yearn for our true home in Heaven. We can further our progress in awakening to our reality by seeing this yearning in everyone, and hearing the same calls for love, peace and freedom, which is a reflection of our true state as spiritual beings in God. Acts of violence can also produce tremendous displays of kindness and compassion when one recognizes the call for love in the violence.

It's now June 7th, 2020. The protests started 12 days ago, and although they started off somewhat violently, they have now become much more peaceful here in Los Angeles. Gary and I were inside our home a few days ago and we started to hear loud chanting, and lots of cars honking their horns. The sound was getting so close until we had to go outside and see what was happening. Turns out that hundreds of people in their cars were driving down our street! We live in a residential neighborhood close to Sunset Blvd., and it was one of the most incredible things I've ever seen. People were chanting "Black Lives Matter," some sitting on top of their cars holding signs, but everyone was cheering with such high energy. I found myself having a spiritual experience in oneness. Something came over me and all the images I was seeing melted away, with no more boundaries between races, no separation, only oneness. Everyone was unified in that moment. It represented the larger unity that we all share with God. This feeling stayed with me for most of the day, and all I could feel was gratitude.

Obviously, most of us know that *all* lives matter and that we *all* equally have the right to be treated with dignity and respect. The point of "Black Lives Matter" is to shed light on the atrocities inflicted on African Americans throughout our history. To deny that this has been a problem wouldn't be very loving. So, at the level of the world, it is perfectly appropriate to stop harmful behavior when possible, while at the same time empowering people to use the anger they feel by channeling it into something positive. This happens when we first correct our misperceptions about ourselves and others to reflect the Holy Spirit's perception. Once we are in our right minds, we can be guided as to the most loving and appropriate actions to take, if any.

An empowering perspective one can hold is to accept that *all* of us have chosen our scripts (or life themes) and in that view there are no victims. These scripts are chosen at another level. We are all working on various themes for the purpose of forgiving ourselves and others and awakening from the dream of separation. Maybe in one illusory lifetime you were the victimizer, so now you are experiencing being the victim. We also change races and genders and have different cultural backgrounds from lifetime to lifetime. Even though reincarnation itself is ultimately an illusion, when you understand that you've been *all* races of people, perhaps there wouldn't be the need to project anger onto others based on their cultural differences or the color of their skin. No matter what happens, we can decide to use our experiences to further our spiritual growth and awaken from the dream; or we can decide to remain victims of the world we made up, further rooting us in the dream. Since the script of time and space is written, it's not really *what* happens that matters, but how we *think* about what happens. The more we think forgiving thoughts and remain in a loving state, the more it is possible to shift to another dimension of time, where we might see the same events, but our experience of it is peaceful. We may even shift to a dimension of time where the event itself is replaced by a gentler scenario. This can happen both on an individual or collective level. **So, you never change the script, for that is written. You do, however, change your *experience* of the script by your choices.**

With all of this going on, I can't help but think that we are experiencing a part of the script where there is a larger ascension process going on — that is, where "old" systems are dying off to allow the new ones to come in. This I would describe as representing our shifting minds in the awakening process. I see all that is happening this year as a reflection of the deeper shifts going on in the mind, manifesting itself in things shifting and changing in the world. Although there still isn't a comprehensive awakening around the world at this time, there is certainly more movement in that direction. It starts with each one of us doing our best to choose right-mindedness, which *is* healing. Right-mindedness corrects wrong-minded thinking so that we can remain above the battleground.

I want to share how I practiced right-minded thinking in a situation that happened in early June, 2020. It was very early in the morning, about 4am, and I got up to use the bathroom. I was still in a dreamy state, and fumbling toward the bathroom door. I slammed into the door, full force! I banged my nose really hard as blood rushed out of me. It really shocked me. Although I was shocked, it should have hurt more, and I was surprised that there was no pain. After taking care of the body part and stopping the bleeding, I immediately said this to myself from the Course, *I am as God created me, His Son can suffer nothing, and I **am** His Son.*[16] I continued with a few right-minded ideas such as "I can decide to be well and choose peace. Suffering is needless. I am having a dream that I am a body that can be hurt, but I am not my body." And from the Course, *The light of truth is in us, where it was placed by God. It is the body that is outside us, and is not our concern.*[17] I turned the situation over to the Holy Spirit, and trusted that He would work on healing the part of my mind that believes in guilt as I went back to sleep. The next morning I felt really good, and only felt a little soreness when I put pressure on my nose. Otherwise, it was as though nothing really happened. I attribute that to the Holy Spirit working its miracle through me. However, a couple days later I started to feel some dizziness. I learned that I had an inner ear concussion, and pressure in the inner ear as a result from my cranial plates being out of alignment was causing the sensation of dizziness. As I write this, I'm still getting treatment for it, and I trust things will unfold for the highest good, as I have let go of what the result has to look like. I recognize the "real" healing involves changing my mind it about through the practice of forgiveness. When I asked Spirit more about the lesson in this, I heard: "Hitting your head was like a metaphor for trying to open your third eye with a truck coming at you full-speed!" In other words, I was being guided to not rush my awakening. Let it happen naturally, with Divine Grace.

This reminds me of a joke: Two spiritual yogis were walking side by side having some sort of intense conversation when one yogi said to the other: "Don't roll your third eye at me."

My process with the above example has been to remember the truth, reinforce right-minded thinking, and letting go of attachment to the outcome. I do this by forgiving and remembering I'm not a body. Although I may have a concussion, and it feels like a rocking sensation inside my head, I'm only dreaming this sensation. I'm taking care of myself by resting, meditating, and taking it easy with screen time (e.g. TV and computer). I was also told by Spirit this would be healed through Craniopathy treatments, which I am now doing. I realize that I'm not really the figure in the dream, but dreaming that I'm a figure in the dream. The object of the game, which is what life is like, is for me to forgive, and not be tempted to make the body my identity. I can choose peace and remember where I really am, home with God. That's what I'm doing. It helps and it works. If I feel some dizziness, I rest while remembering the truth, which makes me happy. I remember I'm not really here, only mentally reviewing that which has already gone by. I will explain how life is like a game, and the instructions on how you can play in a later chapter.

The State of Grace

I will end this chapter with a message from the Holy Spirit on the state of Grace, which I received when I asked for more information on what it means, and this is what was channeled through me:

"Grace is your natural state of being as you remember God. How willing are you to be able to say "God...I only want you." In the state of grace, you are free within the Will of the Divine. You are

free to love wholly and completely. Instead of fearing love, you embrace it as part of yourself. What is given you is not something to be earned, only accepted. For your worthiness is beyond needing to earn. Your worthiness is beyond what you made (the world) and is accepted in the Mind of God that knows Its wholeness.

By grace I live. By grace I am released.[18] *These lines express your complete freedom that returns to your awareness as you continue to practice removing the barriers to it. Do not think of yourself with the littleness of the ego, that is not what you are. You are beyond magnificent. As you let the light of grace shine upon you, and breathe it into your being, you will know the beauty that is you, and then through your release will release all your brothers with you.*

Answer the call to grace and you will remember that you are the light of the world along with your brother and sisters, and the Mind of the Son of God as one will return to its creator and will be fully understood as understanding returns to the Son.

So let's not worry about the end then, for that is certain, but prepare your mind to experience this certainty by recognizing the opportunities that knock on your inner door, for these are the opportunities that will remind you to choose again where you are putting your faith. Put your faith in the world, and you will get the world. Put your faith in God and you will know God was never something you needed to get, but only to accept.

You are alive in God now, for the past is over, and the future never born. Never forget this…for this is the state of grace."

Page for Personal Notes

CHAPTER 6

RELATIONSHIPS FOR THE PURPOSE OF HEALING: SPECIAL VS. HOLY

*Everyone on earth has formed special relationships,
and although this is not so in Heaven, the Holy Spirit
knows how to bring a touch of Heaven to them here.*[1]

When I first met Gary, I had just gotten divorced from my first husband, Steve. I wasn't looking for another relationship at that time. It just happened naturally. I truly felt that I would be single for a long time to allow myself time to be with myself, and be a free Spirit. Another marriage was the last thing on my mind. I realized pretty quickly that my own ideas of what I thought was best for me weren't what the Holy Spirit had in mind. The script is written. You will meet those people you are meant to meet, and will have the opportunity to make all your special relationships holy ones. I fell in love with Gary very quickly, and we knew we wanted to be together, so my ideas of being on my own were completely wiped out. That's what happens when you fall in love. There's not much you can do about it except go with it if the circumstances are right. In our case, when we met, both our marriages were ending and it was Divine timing.

When I think of romantic, worldly relationships, I often joke to myself that if we only loved each other the way love songs say we do, we'd all be on the fast track home! We do feel this love at the beginning of relationships because we are "in love" and so we tend to see only the beautiful aspects of the person at first. Further, we tend to present our best selves to the other person at the beginning, being careful to not make mistakes or embarrass ourselves unnecessarily. We are also very conscious of ourselves and how we look, eat, and dress in front of the other. After some time has passed, that need to be perfect dims, but the unconscious guilt starts coming to the surface the more we get to know someone, and especially when we live with them. This is when things can really get vicious. As Buddha put it, "The tongue, like a sharp knife, kills without drawing blood." We tend to go back and forth between love and hate, and this can't be true love. The ego loves another in order to get something in return. This is the home of the "special" relationship. I found a humorous example of this slow progression from special love to special hate in the following cartoon expressing the difference between how you act when you date and when you are in an actual relationship: "When dating you might say to the other, "HAHAHAHA! Oh, my God! You are so funny!" When in a relationship it becomes, "Is everything a f---ing joke to you!"

Love, as it really is, doesn't need to do anything to be itself. It's just pure, unconditional love. There is no need to get validation or approval from others, and judgment is non-existent. The pure love of God, which represents absolute reality, is not present in this world. However, this love can be expressed in the world through forgiveness. Forgiveness is love in action, but as long as we have a need for forgiveness, it is still not within the realm of perfect love.

The Holy Relationship

The holy relationship *is* the forgiven relationship, where it is understood that our relationships can serve the purpose of the Holy Spirit, learning we are all innocent, and we all call out for love as well as express love. In situations where we are triggered with our partners, we would know that our classroom is in session, and that the "outside picture" (the person) is reflecting back to us what we need to forgive within ourselves. This is why all relationships are blessings and can only be helpful when they are used for this purpose.

As long as we invest in things having to happen a certain way, or the need for people to behave a certain way, we will not be in peace. Experiencing true peace has nothing to do with what is happening on the outside. Remember, the outside picture is irrelevant to being peaceful. Peace is a state of mind that comes when guilt is undone, which means we wouldn't have a need to project that guilt onto others. How joyful and peaceful our relationships can become when we let go of the need to judge! In practice, it is helpful to have the following mindset from the Course: *Have faith in your brother in what but seems to be a trying time. The goal* **is** *set. And your relationship has sanity as its purpose.*[2] This mindset happens when we begin to shift what our relationships are for, from the limited perceptions of others as bodies, to seeing beyond the body as the Great Rays shine from them. This shift to vision happens in the Holy Instant; the instant we choose the Holy Spirit's perception instead of the egos.

The only relationships we "truly" have within the split mind are our relationship with the ego (the only special relationship) and our relationship with Jesus or the Holy Spirit (the only holy relationship). All other relationships are but shadows of these two. The special relationships that seem to take place here, given a holy purpose, can lead us back to our mind and to our mistaken decision to dissociate from the holiness and love in our right mind.

As long as we hold the wrong mind apart from the right mind we're protecting its seeming reality. It is only when we finally bring our decision for the wrong mind to the right mind, ending dissociation from it, that the unreality of the wrong mind is recognized, and dissolves into the nothingness from which it came. This process is called the holy relationship. Its culmination is the "real world," beyond the split mind, where there is no right or wrong mind to choose between, and the decision-maker itself disappears, no longer being necessary or relevant. This makes way for one-mindedness and the fullness of love.

Spiritual partnership is quite different from two people who are married in the traditional sense. You can be married and also be in spiritual partnership, or you can be married without it. When two people come together, not out of lack, but in genuine interest to enjoy each other's company, with the understanding they have come together to make their relationship holy, that is a spiritual partnership. Otherwise, the ego will dominate the relationship and projection will become the basis for it. This can be tricky, but if just one person in the relationship understands this, it can work, although it's a bit more difficult. I am speaking here about any form of relationship, not only romantic partners. These ideas can be applied to any relationship you are experiencing.

People often ask Gary and me whether we have fights. My answer is always the same: "We sometimes disagree, but we don't have loud arguments that last a long time. We both know how to forgive, so an annoyance about a disagreement doesn't last very long. We just accept it and move on, sometimes in just minutes." Maybe things just flow for us because Gary has accepted the "Two Golden Rules to A Happy Marriage:

1. The wife is always right.
2. When you feel she is wrong, slap yourself and read rule number 1 again."

I'm kidding (but seriously) Gary and I have given our relationship to the Holy Spirit to use for *His* purposes. As a result, we have a lot of fun, even though we spend 24 hours together. Things seem to flow, but it doesn't mean everything is perfect all the time. We realize we have a strong purpose in our work together with the Course. Although we teach it to others, we know our job is to apply it in our own lives. When we are teaching others, we are also learning. It's a win-win situation!

The ego's voice can be very loud, and usually dominates until we become more aware of our ego thoughts, which can be vicious. The ego sees the holy relationship as a threat to its existence. Try not to listen to the ego. The Course says:

When you feel the holiness of your relationship is threatened by anything, stop instantly and offer the Holy Spirit your willingness, in spite of fear, to let Him exchange this instant for the holy one that you would rather have. He will never fail in this.[3]

Whoever is saner at the time the threat is perceived should remember how deep is his indebtedness to the other and how much gratitude is due him, and be glad that he can pay his debt by bringing happiness to both. Let him remember this, and say: I desire this holy instant for myself, that I may share it with my brother, whom I love. It is not possible that I can have it without him, or he without me. Yet it is wholly possible for us to share it now.

And so I choose this instant as the one to offer to the Holy Spirit, that His blessing may descend on us, and keep us both in peace.[4]

I guess you could just say, "Holy Spirit, you've got this!" However, I prefer the above ideas, especially when a situation occurs that may require more inner work to return to a state of peace.

What is being offered to us in the Course is a whole new way of thinking about people and the world. We are so trained to believe we understand where our suffering comes from. It's actually the opposite. Instead of people and the world being the cause of our problems, it's actually our mind's choice in how we are looking at it that is the problem. The world is done and over. This means that whatever is happening is part of the script. Our freedom is in choosing how we perceive it *now*. Each moment is a new birth, and we get to choose to see it with fresh eyes, free of the past.

The Special Relationship

"A senior monk and a junior monk were traveling together. At one point, they came to a river with a strong current. As the monks were preparing to cross the river, they saw a very young and beautiful woman also attempting to cross. The young woman asked if they could help her cross to the other side. The two monks glanced at one another because they had taken vows not to touch a woman. Then, without a word, the older monk picked up the woman, carried her across the river, placed her gently on the other side, and carried on his journey.

The younger monk couldn't believe what had just happened. After rejoining his companion, he was speechless, and an hour passed without a word between them.

Two more hours passed, then three, finally the younger monk couldn't contain himself any longer, and blurted out "As monks, we are not permitted to touch a woman, how could you then carry that woman on your shoulders?"

The older monk looked at him and replied, "Brother, I set her down on the other side of the river, why are you still carrying her?"

This powerful parable came to my attention recently, and it sums up very well how we tend to hold onto our past grievances and then project them onto other people. This is the epitome of the special relationship. How often do we all do this? We keep carrying around past upsets and drag them into the present. This is why we are never really in the present moment. The present moment is free of baggage. The ego needs to carry this baggage around for the ego to exist. What does that tell us? If there were no grievances, judgments, or guilt, there would be no "*us*." That is death to the ego because it's invested in separation and differences. This is the home of special relationships.

There is a reason we are attracted to the special love relationship, which is really a mask over special hate. It's a substitute for God's love. The special love relationship obscures from us the understanding that we are powerfully attracted to God. This is the only love that can satisfy us. Let's take a moment and observe how well the special relationship has worked for us. Are you one hundred percent happy, free of conflict, and without any doubts about anything whatsoever? Have you found yourself in what you thought was the relationship of your dreams and found that it has left you wanting more? Do you try to change or fix another's behavior so *you* can be happy? Do you realize that whenever you seem to get everything you want there is still a void or feeling of lack? Is anything enough? If you've answered yes to any of these questions, the special relationship is present in your life.

Our special love and hate relationships are a product of guilt. *The sick attraction of guilt must be recognized for what it is. For having been made real to you, it is essential to look at it clearly, and by withdrawing your investment in it, to learn to let it go. No one would choose to let go what he believes has value. Yet the attraction of guilt has value to you only because you have not looked at what it is, and have judged it completely in the dark. As we bring it to light, your only question will be why it was you ever wanted it.*[5] This passage is telling us that we need to look at the guilt before it can be undone because we have made it real. When we make something real we are giving it value. Once we start questioning our choice for guilt and see clearly what it is bringing us, we wouldn't want to choose it anymore. This takes practice. We are learning to give up what is valueless (guilt, which further roots us in the dream) and keep what is valuable (forgiveness, which awakens us from the dream).

We are so invested and attached to our identities in the world that we spend most of our days in the "outer" world rather than the "inner." We become distracted from the things that would truly give our lives meaning. Another cartoon I read sums up the point of how eager we are to feed our identity as an ego, and place more importance on worldly things than our spiritual growth. A man with a briefcase walked up to a guru, who was meditating, and he said to the guru, "What's the meaning of life? But make it quick, I've got an important meeting in half an hour."

When we look only to our bodily identity to fulfill our sense of lack, we will feel lonely and deprived. The Course explains to us that communication is between minds, not bodies. Communication with the Holy Spirit will restore to you your true ability to give and receive love if you let Him. Loneliness is a product of identification with the body as your reality. It can be overcome by the practice of identifying yourself as a perfect creation of God, Holy in His sight. You cannot lose this connection, but it requires a shift in focus to start training your mind to accept it. When you do, you won't be lonely. What makes us happy is recognizing we are still as God created us, despite the beliefs we have to the contrary.

The reason that bodies are not the source of communication is that *The body is the symbol of the ego, as the ego is the symbol of the separation. And both are nothing more than attempts to limit communication, and thereby to make it impossible. For communication must be unlimited in order to have meaning, and deprived of meaning, it will not satisfy you completely. Yet it remains the only means by which you can establish real relationships, which have no limits, having been established by God.*[6] We need to look at the interference of the ego's perception, which is a limit on real communication, so we can allow the Holy Spirit's perception to inspire our minds. When that happens all judgment is set aside, which means the past is gone. You can't have judgment without the past. The Course puts it this way:

> *Judgment always rests on the past, for past experience is the basis on which you judge. Judgment becomes impossible without the past, for without it you do not understand anything. You would make no attempt to judge, because it would be quite apparent to you that you do not understand what anything means. You are afraid of this because you believe that without the ego, all would be chaos. Yet I assure you that without the ego, all would be love.*[7] This statement is a direct corollary to Workbook Lesson 7 in the Course: *I see only the past.*[8]

So how does this apply to our relationships? We have been trained by the ego to stay rooted in the past, because our first experience of the past is associated with the idea that we sinned against God. That thought got projected out, and now the whole world is caught in a dream of our "sinful past." Of course this is not true, but we unconsciously believe it to be true. All our relationships reflect it. All our beliefs are rooted in time, which has a past, present, and future. These ideas can be difficult to change, but they *must* be changed to be free of the dream of time. An example: When we are with people we know, everything we think or believe about them is based on our past experience of them. So do we really see them for who they are in truth? When we meet people for the first time, those whom we would call strangers, we don't have any preconceived ideas since we don't have any past experience with them. There is no story to attach them to. You may want to practice these ideas in Lesson 7 with your current relationships. This exercise might also be very helpful with any memories of abuse you may be experiencing. Try to see the person in a new light, without a story attached. With practice, what you will see will be so beautiful, untouched, and innocent.

There is no better use for time than learning you are innocent. You can do this through your relationships, no matter what their form. Since the outside world is your projection, and since your body's eyes do see a world, the work is to be mindful of how you are thinking about it. Pull back the lens and try to see the whole picture before you. Be an observer. Most of us still try to single out certain parts of the dream and make them special and different than other parts. When you see the whole picture, you can begin to see that everything is the same. They are all images you have made to take the place of truth. Separation is the great deceiver in all things. When you see another body, you actually think that you are apart from it. That is a trick. You are dreaming of others bodies' just as you are dreaming yours. The "you" who is dreaming outside time and space is still not the *real* you as long as you are dreaming. The one mind that dreams also needs to be returned to God where there is no split; only oneness, wholeness, that which cannot be divided and subdivided over and over again.

The way to remember God is by not making the dream and dream figures real, and remembering who your brothers and sisters really are. They are not apart from you, and all of us are part of God. The Course says that we can delay our progress all we want, but why would we want to if we knew the joy that awaits us? When you become detached from the dualistic world, and you don't need "good" things to happen over "bad" things, you have become free of the world. For all things "good" or "bad" are still part of the dream, and have nothing to do with your worthiness as a Son of God. Peace is a state of mind that requires nothing or no conditions in order for it to *be*. Peace is natural, just like love.

There is a script for every decision you make. There is nothing that occurs that is not part of a script that has been written. When you choose the ego, whatever plays out will serve your ego. When you choose the Holy Spirit, whatever plays out will reflect it as well, not necessarily in form, but in your experience.

I think it's important to remember that just because our relationships here in the world default to "special," it doesn't mean we should avoid relationships, because we *can* transform them into holy relationships. In fact, knowing the purpose of the ego, we can be more watchful for the temptation to project onto others. The ego will look at your attempt to let go of judgment and take responsibility for your feelings as a threat to its existence. Sometimes a relationship may first go through what seems like more conflict at first; this is a defense against the truth. Try to practice seeing it with the understanding that the ego will try to fight you. You don't have to "give in" to its games. Just keep your eye on the goal.

We have all been trained to try and solve problems where they can't be solved. Let's think in terms of relationships, no matter what the form of your relationship. Let's say you are having an issue with someone. That person isn't really the problem, and the solution to the problem is also not found in trying to change that person or the world. Problems aren't made or solved in the world. The world is never the problem. Does this idea make you uncomfortable? If it does, just allow yourself to look at it without judgment. The mind is both the source of problems and the answer, according to which teacher you are listening to. *The ego seeks to "**resolve**" its problems, not at their source, but where they were not made. And thus it seeks to guarantee there will be no solution. The Holy Spirit wants only to make His resolutions complete and perfect, and so He seeks and finds the source of problems where it is, and there undoes it. And with each step in His undoing is the separation more and more undone, and union brought closer.*[9] Here we find again that the only purpose for healing our relationships is union, to see our interests as not separate from someone else's, and to recognize we are all ONE. This is also a reminder to remember that the cause of our upsets is never outside us. We are minds, not bodies. When everything in your life is observed from this point of view, you can truly be in charge of how you experience your life. That is true power.

Special Relationships with Things

Special relationship's aren't limited to people. There are many things we form special relationship's with, including but not limited to, mind altering substances, shopping, gambling, and food to name a few. These are also substitutes for God's love. If we look closely, these are pretty shabby substitutes because anything you find yourself addicted to means you need it *because* it is not true. We don't need what we already are, which is love. A solution at the mind level for being addicted to things is to practice giving up the teacher of addiction, the ego, and switch to the teacher of the Holy Spirit. If you believe genetics plays a role then it would be helpful to deal with that level as well. In truth, if the body is in the mind, then the mind has control over what it thinks and believes, so therefore you can work at that level and get very positive results.

I used to have a special relationship with dark chocolate, but I didn't make myself guilty for eating it. I do eat it on occasion, but without guilt. It's the guilt that hurts us, not the form of whatever you have made the special relationship with. On one occasion, I did have a guilty "puppy face" when I was craving some chocolate, and Gary had some of his favorite chocolate bars in a kitchen drawer. I gave in to my ego and ate his chocolate! Later, he went for that drawer only to discover his wonderful chocolate was gone. He was really looking forward to it. I went up to him with my "puppy face" and said "I'm so sorry I ate your chocolate." He said in a gentle, but somewhat disappointing tone, "That's okay, baby, I understand." That produced more guilt than eating the chocolate would have! So, I went out and bought him more chocolate and he smiled. He also didn't make it a big deal, and then said to me that he understood, because when he was a child, his mother loved eclairs. One night he ate his mother's eclairs, and when she went to the refrigerator to get them, she was so disappointed to find them gone. I know this is a simple example, and we always joke about this with each other now, but it's the point behind it that matters. The point is that guilt never serves us. Also, when it comes to the topic of food in general, it's almost impossible not to have beliefs attached to it to some degree. All of us have things we believe are healthier than other things, and then we have things that we believe are not healthy. The point is as long as you hold onto beliefs about something, it would serve you to follow them. If you truly believed nothing would hurt you, and that you aren't a body, then nothing would hurt you.

This brings up a subject I'd like to address that I feel is important. There are many ways we make the world real. We make it real by strongly opposing something, and also pretending like people aren't suffering because we know the world is an illusion, so we deny the suffering. Both of these mindsets make the world real. I'd like to use an example. As I write this, the world is still in the middle of the covid-19 pandemic. In our city of Los Angeles, it has been a requirement that we wear masks whenever we go out in public. If not, you could be fined. Whatever you believe about the pandemic itself is irrelevant to the following point. I've seen both sides of the coin, those that strongly oppose wearing masks and those that strongly support it. Whichever side you are on, the point is when anyone strongly opposes something such as saying "You won't catch me wearing a mask" even though it is required and it is clearly making others uncomfortable when you don't wear one, that is making the world just as real as if you are terrified of getting sick so you become obsessive about others wearing a mask. Both make the world real. My opinion is that although I don't prefer to wear a mask, I do it when in public because it's a way of joining with others, especially when it seems clear that the majority of people appreciate it when you do. It's the principle behind it. The ego is tricky, and a strong opposition against something is a sign that the ego is in action. This doesn't mean you shouldn't have firm opinions or not take action on things, but your attitude and behavior would come from a calm, peaceful mindset instead of anger and fear.

How to Know Whether or Not to Stay In or End a Relationship

In special relationships, it is very common to identify with another's problems in such a way that you take them on as if they were yours. This is a mistake, and the result is unnecessary suffering. This is the ego's way of identifying with the dream, which makes it real. In many ways it seems loving to do this, but it's really hurting all parties involved because it keeps the separation going. A helpful thing to do in these situations is to make sure you are in your right mind when another is having a problem. Get centered first, before you speak with the person. This way you can guide and assist from a loving and understanding place, which is true empathy, rather than sympathizing, which makes the problem real to both of you. If the person you are with is someone very close to you, such as a family member, friend, or spouse, which means there are attachments you have to the person, then there is often an opportunity for tremendous growth and healing. Therefore, one should be clear what purpose the relationship is serving, and whether or not you have honored that relationship completely before you decide to end it or leave. This means that it's better to work out and heal what needs to be healed within yourself with that person, or else you might later regret it. Also, if it is not dealt with, the guilt will just get projected out in another form with another person.

Not taking on another person's problems doesn't mean you lose interest in them and pretend there is nothing going on, especially if it's a personal relationship. This can be challenging, because if the other person is in their ego, they will do everything they can to manipulate you to take their side, or to convince you it's your fault. If you are also in your ego when this happens, it produces a vicious, never-ending cycle of fear. Perhaps the lesson in this is that you are learning that it's okay to have boundaries, not allowing people to dominate or control you. Again, this can be worked out with love in your mind instead of judgment.

If you are still feeling that you may want to end or leave a relationship, you might try asking yourself what your role is in the relationship, and is the relationship an essential part of your life moving forward. If you feel it is very essential to your life in some way, it may be best to heal what needs to be healed before you leave. You may even find a win-win situation with the person and end up staying. If the relationship is not essential to your life, then the practice would be to honor your choice to remove yourself from it without guilt. Watch out for the trickiness of the ego in having you immediately remove yourself as soon as something starts to feel uncomfortable, especially at the beginning of a relationship. All relationships include things that are uncomfortable. Just because something feels uncomfortable might not mean it's best to walk out, unless it's coming from clear guidance having to do with being in danger in some way.

Instead, try to understand the purpose of the relationship in your life. Inquire more about what it has to teach you. If you have a clear understanding of that, you can leave the relationship in peace. If you attempt to leave just because you had one fight or you feel a bit uncomfortable, that is more of an escape from one's own inner problems. Then, you are likely to find yourself in another relationship that has similar problems, because the problem wasn't really solved in the former relationship. Remember, the problem is rarely the other person. It's our own mind's choice for choosing the ego's interpretation that is the problem, which started with the original separation from God. From the Course's perspective, all problems have been solved because the separation has been solved. Most of us aren't quite there yet in accepting this. So, the next best thing is to work on forgiving the content in our own minds that is upsetting to us, which means we are taking full responsibility for our thoughts and feelings.

Sometimes we demand so many things from our partners, asking for the impossible, instead of accepting them for who they are. Here's some relevant humor:

"Two women were having a conversation about relationships, and one woman said to the other, 'I want a man who's loyal, faithful, patient, attentive, forgiving, unselfish, even-tempered and a good listener!' The other woman flatly replied, "You mean you want a dog."

Sorry, men, if my jokes are not balanced. Here is one for the men: "A woman is about to approach her partner for a discussion on their relationship, and the man senses this and gently says, 'Let's not complicate our relationship by trying to communicate with each other.'"

The Power to Choose

Love is the "missing ingredient" in most exchanges, and instead of *love* being the underlying inspiration for communication, it is usually the ego. The Course says, *Trust not your good intentions. They are not enough.*[10] In other words, ask yourself before any interaction, what is the purpose of this? Remember to clarify your goal at the beginning. Otherwise, the ego is usually the default mode we are in until we remember to change our minds.

Let us all remember that there is only a *belief* in the ego, which is darkness. Choosing the Holy Spirit (the right part of your mind that is the answer to the separation) is choosing the light. We can remember that we always have a choice in how we are looking at everything, and how we are thinking of everything. You do not have to settle for the ego's interpretation of your life, relationships, health, work, etc. It's just an interpretation, not a fact. If you are upset or unsettled by anything, and a sense of uncertainty enters your mind, remember that the cause of the upset is a choice in your mind, just as the remedy is also in your mind. **Whether the issue you are having is about a relationship, health, finances, or anything else, remember to repeat to yourself often that you are a strong, certain, all-powerful, and invulnerable Spirit.** It does help to think this way, and as long as you have a choice, it can produce positive results to entertain these ideas in your mind instead of the alternative.

Knowing that there is another way to think about problems when there is an upset is giving you back your freedom to choose. It is remembering the truth about you and everyone; that we are all innocent, children of God. Please try to remember that those who call out for love are doing the best they can with the awareness they have at the time, even if they seem vicious. *Forgive them for they know not what they do.* This doesn't mean we have to be passive to horrific events, but we can think of people and the world with correct perception, staying vigilant for the truth. God didn't create us as bodies, but as an extension of His Love.

It takes willingness, patience, and practice to stay vigilant only for God, and to stay on the path of awakening together by being kind and forgiving to all our brothers and sisters who are on this path together as ONE. When we use the past to judge others it hides their reality from your sight. Light, Truth, God, Oneness is in the eternal NOW, not in the past. Just because something is being experienced in time, doesn't make it real.

The way out of suffering in our relationships and in the world is to recognize that what we are seeing with the body's eyes isn't reality. It's a limited perception that we keep making real by our belief in it. The Course says that if we see people as they really are as Christ, whole and innocent, we will understand that Christ has no past, for He is changeless (still whole, perfect love - all of us as One as God Created us) and in His changelessness lies your release. For if He is as He was created, there is no guilt in Him, which means there is none in you. We are afraid of light (truth) because it means the end of the ego, the self we have identified with for many illusory eons! We can keep forgiving ourselves and being gentle with ourselves, with a gentle smile and humor, remembering to not take ourselves and the world too seriously, while still being helpful here.

Whenever I am making any relationship special, it is helpful for me to remember that time can be used to imprison myself as well as free myself, depending on my interpretation. Judge the world not, and it will not judge you. Judge the world, and you will be judged. This is because there is only ONE of us, although it seems like 7 billion different minds! As you see another, you see yourself. When you wake up from a dream in bed in the morning...do you judge the figures in your dream and make them real? Do you get upset at the figures in your dream? Most likely the answer is no because you know the dream wasn't real, and to attack or get angry at the figures in the dream and judge them would be insane because we made them up. Well, that is like this dream, when we appear to be awake. If this is also a form of dreaming, then to attack, judge, condemn and blame the people that we made up in this form of dreaming is no different...it is also insane. It's tricky because this is not our experience, but through forgiveness the belief in the ego is undone more and more, and then eventually we will all just experience our reality. There is no need to try and get there faster, just practice forgiving those things that disturb you on a daily basis. Step by step, thought by thought, and you are working your way to true freedom!

We are asked to gradually let go of all concepts of the self, all images we hold about ourselves, emptying our minds of everything it thinks it knows or understands; to let go of the past and all the beliefs we've learned, so that we won't make the mistake of using the past as the light to guide us now. When we can catch ourselves when we are not feeling at peace, we can then gently remind ourselves that we must have chosen wrongly, and we can decide otherwise. Ask the Holy Spirit to be your guide in seeing. This is what it means to put the Holy Spirit in charge.

Experiencing ourselves in the world doesn't mean we should try and make a perfect world, for that is impossible. We can be normal. However, we can experience perfect forgiveness and perfect peace, which comes from true forgiveness. We can do our best to remember that we can decide how we want to feel and how we interpret something. Every time I remember to do that, I feel better. That is what I keep reinforcing in my mind. In the Course, Jesus says we only see what we wish to see and that is all. That alone is the reason for how we feel. **The mind thinks a thought it wishes to have, then it makes an image, that image gets projected out, and then that image is what we think is real.** If you trace it back, you can see it's the thoughts we have that make everything real first, but gets projected out so that we think the screen is what needs to be changed, which is what the ego wants us to think. So by changing the thought and interpretation at the mind level, then we will understand that images mean nothing, and that even the thought behind it meant nothing if it's coming from ego. This is truly exercising the power of the mind!

Please know you are loved, holy, and in the Mind of God. You cannot be anything else or be anywhere else. Any other interpretation of ourselves and our brothers and sisters is false and doesn't exist. You are as God created you. You remember God by thinking of everyone else as nothing less than God. Jesus says in the Course that He has perfect faith in you to do all that you would accomplish. He means that by seeing all your brothers and sisters as the Christ, you will gain the benefits of understanding that this is what you are. This is your identity as established by God, and you cannot fail in this. If you are dealing with a difficult relationship, it may be helpful to say the following words to yourself from the Course:

I give you to the Holy Spirit as part of myself. I know that you will be released, unless I want to use you to imprison myself. In the name of my freedom I choose your release, because I recognize that we will be released together.[11]

We all have challenges from time to time in our relationships, and we are not asked to deny these experiences, but to forgive them. **As we forgive others by over-looking the errors we see from the beginning, we will realize that those errors have already been replaced by Holy Spirit's Atonement principle that says nothing happened. You are still innocent, and sin does not exist. It is only a belief, and beliefs can be undone. That is the work of the Course...salvation is undoing...undoing what never was.**

I often think about my relationship with Gary, and how different my perception of it is now than it was at the beginning. I was much more insecure and possessive at the beginning. I have learned that I am with Gary, not because I *need* him, but because I *enjoy* being with him. I have freed him in my mind from anything my ego wants to control. This has allowed me to experience my relationship with him in a whole new way. Love doesn't own or possess, it frees the other to be as they are without judgment. In other words, love is consistent. It won't change even when we try to change it. This is why the pure love of God is not found in the world. The world is not built on unconditional love, but was made with special love. Once again, love is expressed in this world through forgiveness. Gary and I often notice that we don't stay upset at each other for very long, because we always remember who the other really is, and we forgive. This isn't always easy, and it can be very hard sometimes, but we feel so much better when we turn it over to the Holy Spirit.

In Lesson 284 in the Course, it's pretty obvious that Jesus knows we will have resistance to changing our minds, and will lose our faith in the Holy Spirit. So he gently reminds us to take it thought by thought until we fully accept it. The lesson, *I can elect to change all thoughts that hurt,* says:

Loss is not loss when properly perceived. Pain is impossible. There is no grief with any cause at all. And suffering of any kind is nothing but a dream. This is the truth, at first to be but said and then repeated many times; and next to be accepted as but partly true, with many reservations. Then to be considered seriously more and more, and finally accepted as the truth. I can elect to change all thoughts that hurt. And I would go beyond these words today, and past all reservations, and arrive at full acceptance of the truth in them.[12]

This amazing lesson can be so helpful when we remember that all of us have resistance to the truth, and it just takes willingness along with repetition of these ideas until we fully accept them into our minds. Many places in the Course, Jesus assures us He has faith in us. So, any time you have doubt about anything, and the world seems to get in your face, and you feel tired and weak…know you are not alone because you are in the Mind of God, even if you don't see it. Remind yourself that you are worthy of the consistent effort it takes to choose again what your reality is, that you don't have to earn your Divinity. It was given to you as a gift. You don't have to earn a gift, only accept it.

Perspectives on Parenting in Relationship to Children

Although *all* our relationships are "special" here until we offer them to the Holy Spirit to use for His purposes, the relationships we have with our children often involve deep bonds and attachments that we cherish; but they also involve a great deal of pain. In working with children, it's very helpful to remember that they are also children of God, and they belong to Him. Many people ask me how they can teach the Course to children. The best way to teach children is to demonstrate its principles by living it the best you can in your everyday life. This involves letting go of judgment on your children, while still guiding, supporting, and disciplining them from a place of love. As a parent, it is your duty to guide and direct until they are old enough to take care of themselves. It's okay to set firm boundaries and discipline your children, but it can be done from an inspired and loving place within you. The best teacher teaches through love, not fear.

I'm sure every parent knows that it can be challenging to discern whether or not your parenting skills are inspired by the Holy Spirit. I would like to offer an example of an approach one can take with one's children when an uncertain or upsetting situation arises, and you don't know what to do. Here is one example of a right-minded way to talk to your child:

"I may not always be right, or even always know what to do, and we may not always see eye to eye, but I do know that I love you, and while you are still a minor, sometimes there are important decisions that need to be made, and as the adult I need to step in and make a decision that might not be to your liking, but it comes from love. At the same time, I do understand that you have your own ideas and thoughts about the way things should be and I respect that, too. Just know that if I need to step in, I am just doing my job as a mother/father who loves her/his child and fulfilling my function until you are old enough to be on your own. There are times I may see it your way, and times when I may not. And because I have lots of life experience I can hold a perspective on certain things that you may not have experienced yet. It is with these ideas that my guidance and decision making can be most loving and helpful whether you know it or not yet."

The above example is an approach that lets your child know you care and love them, and that you support them while also respecting the idea that they have their own perspective, whether you agree with it or not. When you are coming from your right mind when you speak to them, whatever you do or say will be loving and helpful.

As a parent, it is also important to check in and stay informed about what is going on with your child whenever you can, but without being too possessive or over-bearing. That can make the child rebel even further. Offer your assistance whenever it is needed and just let the child know you are always there for them if they need to talk, and give them a safe outlet for expressing their feelings. Just listen. Try and watch the temptation to over-ride what they say with quick opposition. Allow them to talk and express themselves. This way, they will develop trust in you to listen without judgment. Most people just want to be "heard." They don't want to be lectured. Listening goes a long way, with both children and adults.

Being Authentic in Your Relationships

Being authentic is important in all of your relationships, including your children. What does it mean to be an authentic? Why is it important? When you are being authentic, your beauty or the essence of the real you shines through, and you become beautiful to everyone because the light/truth is attractive. People are drawn to the light. So, you don't' have to do anything to fix the form/body, rather change your mind about what it means to be authentic and that will help you feel more connected to Spirit. This means being really honest with yourself about your thoughts and feelings, and watching the temptation to project onto others, while extending your love instead. Authenticity radiates from within, and then extends itself so that others feel permission to be authentic, too, in your presence.

This is important because there is only beauty and truth within you, and that is what is real. So, when you get in touch with that and realize that it has nothing to do with what is external, you don't have to be at the effect of the world's projections.

Tips on being authentic

1. Identify yourself as Spirit, connect with that part of you, and practice letting go of attachment to body identification, and making that your reality. The body is just an image, and it has nothing to do with what you are. Whichever teacher we choose to identify ourselves with in the mind will then produce the experience we have in the outside world. Being authentic requires awareness. You will feel as authentic as your thoughts about yourself. How are you thinking of yourself? Be aware of that.
2. Practice letting the love of the Holy Spirit extend through you. What can be more beautiful and authentic than that?

3. To express your authenticity, practice letting go of attachment to your ego. The Course trains the mind how to do this. The ego is nothing more than a belief about yourself, an image that we have all made real. The image is a projection coming from the mind. The real you is the authentic you, which is perfect Spirit. Get in touch with this and invest your faith in Spirit, and you will be free; free from an image that looks back at you in the mirror telling you that you are not a Holy Son of God. An image isn't you. **You are in the Mind that created you, and it created you perfect. You are being breathed by God. Think of that to remind yourself that you are always Holy.**

Loneliness

There may be nothing more devastating than the experience of feeling lonely and living without a clear purpose in mind. Masses of people experience loneliness at one time or another, and if it's left to the ego to judge, it can make things worse. The good news is that there is something that can be done about this, because loneliness is a state of mind that can be changed when one's will is aligned with God's will, which is that we be happy and in a state of peace. If you are experiencing loneliness, the first error that can be corrected is the belief that you need other people physically to be with you in order to not feel lonely. Many people feel lonely because they are not in a relationship with someone, and so they attribute their loneliness to that being the cause. As a Course student, it can be very helpful to remember that nothing outside you has the power to affect you in any way unless you give it that power. This puts you at *cause,* and in charge of your thoughts.

The root cause of feeling lonely is an effect of a thought (often disguised) that says "I am apart from God. I lost Him. Now I am all alone." The ego's answer to this is to find a false sense of oneness in which we seek out those people who think like us, even if they make fun of other people or are judgmental, so we won't feel so alone. This is the ego's twisted way of joining. It can feel very real, and as I said can be a devastating experience once we realize what we are doing and that it's not making us happy. Non-judgment of the self is very important when feeling this way. Allow yourself to feel the loneliness without judgment the best you can. When you can become the observer of yourself, it places you above the battleground so you can start to recognize you are much greater than your body, and even your thoughts and feelings. This means, you are observing yourself with the Holy Spirit or Jesus holding your hand, looking at it with you. This can be a very comforting experience. Forgiveness of self and forgiving the projection of loneliness is also an important part of this process. The idea is to start identifying with God as your reality, and letting ego identification with the body go. This doesn't mean you are literally neglecting the body, but you are not making the body your reality, since the body represents a limit on awareness.

When you remember that you are mind, you can expand your thinking and imagine yourself anywhere you wish to be, and that includes how you are thinking about things. This is very powerful and has tremendous benefits whether you see them right away or not. Also, having healthy, holy relationships starts with the relationship you have with the Holy Spirit. Once you start identifying with Spirit as your reality, the special relationship with the ego will melt away.

To summarize, the key to working with all relationships and the emotions and feelings that surround them, is to get very clear first on what purpose we want our relationships to serve for us. When we turn them over to the Holy Spirit, they become beautiful classrooms for learning we are all innocent. This requires forgiving the guilt that drives these special relationships so they become holy, in which we would see God in all our brothers, and therefore in ourselves. When we have this clear goal in mind, there is nothing more to do. The Holy Spirit will be your guide as you continue to trust and remain open to Him, letting go of attachments to outcomes.

Since the script is written, it matters not *what* happens, but how you *think* about what happens. This is not always easy, but possible with willingness, patience and practice. I've heard from countless people how tired they are of the world and want to go home. I understand that feeling, but I also understand that you can be so happy and peaceful that the timing of when it's your turn to be enlightened doesn't matter. That is the point. If we dwell on the need to wake up and try to purposely rush the process, it is also making the world very real for ourselves, and we may even hurt ourselves in the process. To want to wake up is a good thing, but just watch your investment in it. Ask yourself if your wanting to wake up is driven by the ego, which means you will be coming from a place of lack in your mind about it. You are always connected to God, and can't lose that connection. Practice patience, as the Course says: *Those who are certain of the outcome can afford to wait, and wait without anxiety. Patience is natural to the teacher of God. All he sees is certain outcome, at a time perhaps unknown to him as yet, but not in doubt.*[13] The outcome the Course speaks of here is love. All your relationships will be transformed from darkness to light, and everything under the sun will look so lovely because your perception has been aligned with the teacher of love, the Holy Spirit.

To close this chapter, I'd like to share one of my favorite expressions of love from Arten and Pursah about what happens when we forgive our special relationships and the world in general:

Each day that you forgive, the effects of all the world's mistakes are melted as snow into a burning fire. No more guilt, no more karma, no more fear of what may be. For you have met yourself and declared your innocence, and all that follows is as natural as God.

Nor more birth, nor old death; these were just ideas. If you should come again to help a few more to find the way, so be it; but you are not a body, you are love, and it matters not where love appears to be. For being love, it cannot be wrong.

The day will come when pain is impossible, love is everywhere, and truth is all there is. You've longed for this forever, often silently and without knowing it. The knowledge of what you are is more certain now, and love has forgotten no one.

The day will come when the world will sing the song of spirit instead of weeping tones that hide the Voice for truth. The day will come when there is nothing left to forgive, and the celebration with your sisters and your brothers is in order.

And then the day will come when there is no more need for days. And you will live as one forever in the holiness of your immortal reality.[14]

Page for Personal Notes

CHAPTER 7

HOW TO SEE WITH
SPIRITUAL SIGHT

*The opposite of seeing through the body's eyes is the vision
of Christ, which reflects strength rather than weakness,
unity rather than separation, and love rather than fear.*[1]

From the day we are born, we are thrust into a world of separation, which is a projection of our "first" experience of separation from God, experienced as being pushed out into the world from our mother's womb. PTSD (post-traumatic stress disorder) can be traced back to this idea. We are literally stressed from this perception of separation. A baby feels terrible and cries when it leaves the cozy, comfortable womb of its mother just as all of us felt terrible over feeling that we separated from God. Later on in life, we then learn to be comfortably numb in a world of pain, so that we don't have to feel the terrible guilt over the separation. This can take the form of numbing ourselves with drugs and alcohol, and other addictive behaviors. These idols we use are substitutes for God's love, because they temporarily provide us relief, but never have lasting effects. Once we catch the addiction train, we are off and running, which is just how the ego wants it. *All* of us are addicted to the ego, which means we all have work to do to switch from the teacher of addiction (the ego) to the teacher of healing (the Holy Spirit).

After the thought of separation *appeared* to occur, instead of being with God in perfect oneness, we now appear to have a body that can seemingly "see" with the body's eyes. Our true vision as Christ was hijacked so that it now becomes the body's eyes that "see" which, as the Course explains, is not really seeing at all. It's image-making. Birth is not really a miracle as some say, although we should allow ourselves to enjoy the event, all the while knowing we are perfect spirit, not bodies. If this idea makes some people sensitive, please forgive me. All we have to do is look closely at the world we made and think to ourselves, "Is the world worthy of being called a miracle?" Also, let's remember that the "miracle" in the Course is not about anything physical. It's a shift in perception that occurs in the mind, shifting from fear to love. Once we are thrust out into an illusory world, it's easy to make it real, because all our senses tell us it's real. Even in our dreams in bed at night, we feel and see things that aren't really there. We even feel sensations in our dreams, which is really the mind that is feeling them, and also seeing the images. Our body's eyes are closed when we sleep, so the mind is still projecting images when we sleep.

Since it is our experience that we are born into a body in a world of time and space, it's best to go along with it and live a "normal" life to the best of our ability. You can still recognize where you really come from. God birthed you as a thought in His Mind, so you belong to *Him*, not the world.

The body's eyes represent a limit on seeing. Seeing something with your body's eyes doesn't mean you understand what you see. Here is how the Course puts it:

These eyes, made not to see, will never see. For the idea they represent left not its maker, and it is their maker that sees through them. What was its maker's goal but not to see? For this the body's eyes rest on externals and cannot go beyond. Watch how they stop at nothingness, unable to go beyond the form to meaning. Nothing so blinding as perception of form. For sight of form means understanding has been obscured.[2]

This is saying that since the ego represents the thought of separation, whatever it makes or projects cannot be real, since its purpose is to keep us mindless. Our bodies eyes stop at form. So we think that the forms and images we see represent the truth. Instead, the Course is asking us to see beyond the form to the true meaning, where true understanding enlightens our minds. Things are not always as they seem. How quick we are to judge what our body's eyes see! The form is nothing. It's the content behind the form that matters.

We are taught that "seeing is believing." It's actually the other way around. "Believing is seeing." We see what we believe is there. We believe we are bodies that have eyes through which we see, so we see things. This doesn't equate with true understanding, and explains why we can't judge anyone truly. However, if we truly believed we were the Son of God, that's all we would see as well; only innocence and perfect spirit. **When we judge someone with our egos, we are saying we understand. This is a lie and hurts our minds.**

Spiritual Sight and the Message of the Crucifixion

Spiritual sight or Vision has nothing to do with the body's eyes, but how you are *thinking* about others. With spiritual sight, we would see only innocence in others, and look past the errors of others to the Christ in all of us. Everyone and everything is seen from a different point of view when there are only calls for love or expressions of love. Love is always the response in the Christ Mind. This is not always easy to practice because we feel justified in our anger towards others as a result of the belief that others can really hurt us.

Let's take a look at how spiritual sight was practiced by Jesus at the Crucifixion. His commentary on his own experience with this historic story paints a very different picture of what his state of mind was like at the time, which reflects the Christ Vision we are talking about. Here are some of the things he said about it, and you will see how he is purely non-dualistic in his thinking, which is the message of the Course:

> *The real meaning of the crucifixion lies in the **apparent** intensity of the assault of some of the Sons of God upon another. This, of course, is impossible, and must be fully understood **as** impossible. Otherwise, I cannot serve as a model for learning.[3]*
>
> *Assault can ultimately be made only on the body. There is little doubt that one body can assault another, and can even destroy it.*

*Yet if destruction itself is impossible, anything that is destructible cannot be real. Its destruction, therefore, does not justify anger. To the extent to which you believe that it does, you are accepting false premises and teaching them to others. The message the crucifixion was intended to teach was that it is not necessary to perceive any form of assault in persecution, because you cannot **be** persecuted. If you respond with anger, you must be equating yourself with the destructible, and are therefore regarding yourself insanely.[4]*

You are free to perceive yourself as persecuted if you choose. When you do choose to react that way, however, you might remember that I was persecuted as the world judges, and did not share this evaluation for myself. And because I did not share it, I did not strengthen it. I therefore offered a different interpretation of attack, and one which I want to share with you. If you will believe it, you will help me teach it.[5]

The message of the crucifixion is perfectly clear: Teach only love, for that is what you are.[6]

When I first read this interpretation, I was so inspired by it. It made a lot of sense to me given the non-dualistic nature of reality. I also recognized what a striking example this is and a powerful lesson for all of us. One who learns to listen *only* to the Holy Spirit would indeed be able to choose to perceive such an extreme situation with unconditional love. Jesus was using this as a call for peace. He says,… *All are called, but few choose to listen. Therefore, they do not choose right. Right minds can do this now, and they will find rest unto their souls. God knows you only in peace, and this **is** your reality.[7]*

We all have a tendency to crucify ourselves in many different ways, and the one cause for all of these forms is the guilt that is unconscious to us, until we make it conscious and forgive it. It would actually serve us well to be as God created us, behaving as if we knew this to be true, but without the ego. This reminds me of a great cat joke that a friend told us about. If you have a cat, like Gary and I do, you may relate to the idea in the following joke:

A German Shepherd, a Doberman, and a cat die and go to heaven. God greets the three and asks each what they believe in. First God asks the German Shepherd, who replies, "I believe in discipline and loyalty to my master." God says, "This is good, you can sit here at my right hand." Next God asks the Doberman what he believes in. The Doberman replies, "I believe in love and protecting my master." God says, "Wonderful, you can sit here at my left." Finally God asks the cat what he believes in, and the cat replies, "I believe you are in my seat."

Luna, our cat, is not shy about letting us know she is a god and must be treated that way! She always gets the best seat in the house, whether we like it or not. Cats just have this attitude about them, like nothing can reduce them to something they are not. Perhaps this is due to the fact that cats were revered as Gods in ancient Egypt, so they have this ancient sense of entitlement. I find it very cool, but also amusing! I love all animals, and have always respected them and their ability to be present, and to adapt to their surrounding environment with ease. My love for animals started back in ancient Atlantis when I was an animal communicator, and I knew the language of the birds. It's no wonder that I love to sing to the animals! People were much more in touch with animals in those times, and also had open communication with E.T.'s.

An Unusual Encounter

Speaking of E.T.'s, they do exist in the illusion. What they want is to bring about another Atlantis where there is open communication and where ideas are shared, such as technology and other resources, working in harmony and remembering we all share the cosmos together. They also want to help us not destroy ourselves and the planet, which seems to be where we are headed much of the time.

There will come a time soon when it is known that they are here, but they won't appear on the White House lawn. They often appear in people's dreams as a way of acclimating us to their presence. In fact, I had a very profound vision of meeting some of them in my dream state and later learned this was an authentic experience of contact. In my vision, Gary and I were standing in a field, and all of a sudden there were many colored lights swirling around us. They were beautiful colors, bright and brilliant. I looked up at the sky and I saw what looked like shooting stars flying by in the sky above us, and there were dozens of them, coming one after another. I said to Gary, excitedly, "Look! Do you see that!" Gary was kind of neutral about it. Then, I found myself sitting in a futuristic-looking vehicle going at a fast speed. Gary was still with me, and in front of us there was another vehicle and I could see inside the windows. There were two beings, one looked reptilian and the other like a grey type of E.T. They were looking at us and were very curious about us, but they were just observing us. Another being, a male who looked very human, sat next to Gary in the back seat. I asked him who he was and he said his name was Mabin. I looked to my right, outside the vehicle window and the two beings I saw in front of us in the other car were now at my right side, just observing us again. I had no fear whatsoever, but I kept saying to Gary, "Look! Do you see them?!" Gary's reaction was neutral again, but I was very excited to see them. Finally, we were riding along and were headed to some facility where we were going to hear someone speak about the nature of the mind. When we arrived, Mabin, the human looking E.T., was still with us. We were standing right beside him and I asked him if I could get a photo with him. He said I could, and he put his arm very gently around me and took my hand and held it with his behind our backs. It was very sweet and gentle. I looked to my right and saw another being, but more like a creature who looked sort of like a dinosaur. It was flying by pretty fast. Lastly, I found myself in some sort of a spaceship, standing in front of what seemed like the controls to navigate the spaceship. I asked the beings, "Are you going to do experiments on me, and will you be kind to me?" Then I woke up, but knew that I had an unusual experience. I had the goosebumps all over and had the feeling I always have when I know I just had a mystical type experience. Later, I found out that this was indeed an authentic E.T. contact, and was told that they were coming to check in with us, to check on our well-being. I apparently knew these beings from Atlantis, and sometimes they do come and check on those beings that have incarnated in their star systems, and that have had a relationship with them in some way.

I share this story not to frighten people, but to show that there are benevolent beings that aren't from this planet, but that have good intentions. The E.T.'s are not here to hurt us, but are another example of the universe of duality. No matter what life form, you will always have those that are well intentioned and those that may have a different agenda, just like on our earth; it's no different. I am encouraged by the possibility that we can have open contact without fear. Again, they are here to join with us, not separate. Many people think they are ready to see them, but if you are really honest with yourself, there is probably some fear there. If you are interested in having contact, you can practice seeing if you are ready by observing images of all kinds of beings and see how you respond to them. There are thousands of different-looking beings in the universe of time and space, and as Arten and Pursah have said, "We should think of them as our brothers and sisters in space." I didn't intend to talk about this, but I always follow what comes naturally, and if it feels inspired then I go with it.

Gary and I recently went on a trip to Yellowstone National Park. I must say that this was one of the most beautiful and peaceful trips we've ever taken together. We stayed at a friend's house in Sheridan, Wyoming, at the start of our trip, and then rented a car and drove to Yellowstone. While in Sheridan, our friend introduced us to the loveliest animals: Her two horses (Sammy and Brio), a goat (Peter), a dog (Merit), a cat (Tweedy) and three hens. What joy I felt being around these light-filled beings! Looking into Merit's eyes was like looking at the Holy Spirit. This dog exuded so much love that I just melted at the sight of her. It was truly a healing experience being around all of them. This is a tribute to our friend, too, for creating such a joyful space to live, where even the animals were joyful.

The scenery on the way to Yellowstone was stunning as we drove through Red Lodge, Montana, and then made our way into the northeast entrance of Yellowstone. We saw Bison, Elk, Moose, a Blue Heron, and a bear during our stay there. The waterfalls, lakes, geysers, and wild life are inspiring. I know it's a dream, but nature can be a part of our happy dream, and we are all truly an extension of nature in the dream, just as all of us as the Son of God are an extension of God in reality. So, we can enjoy the beauty, and still remember that it's a reflection of our right minds in the dream.

Our first day driving into Yellowstone, we passed a very large field filled with Bison. A few of them started walking toward our car and onto the road right in front of us. They are very large and unique-looking beings. Of course I started singing to them. As I said, I love to sing to animals. They respond very positively to singing. Usually they look at me with curiosity. I doubt that any of the Bison in Yellowstone have people singing to them very often! But it was fun. Gary didn't hold back from reminding me that this wasn't a petting zoo. If you can, I highly recommend making a trip to see this gorgeous national park. You won't be disappointed.

My excitement throughout the trip was apparent to the point where I almost apologized to Gary for being so happy! Of course I know I don't need to apologize for that, but I was off the charts happy and excited about being in the energy of the park and around the animals. I also remember Arten saying never to apologize from a place of feeling guilty. You can apologize as a way of taking responsibility for a mistake you feel needs correction on your part, but you can do it while still knowing you are innocent in truth. So here is my point: When you are super excited and happy, and follow your joy, that is also the Holy Spirit communicating through you or your intuition speaking to you that you are in a pure state of being. It is natural for us to be in a state of joy, and it's okay to enjoy beauty in the world. I always remember that I choose to be happy first, and then it's reflected in the things around me. Also, there is a way to be happy without being attached to the images we see, which reflects the awareness that only God is what truly makes us happy. Even when I get excited I am fully aware of this idea. Sometimes I practice an exercise where I retain the joy, but drop the images in my mind that seem to bring about the joy. This way I am telling my mind that I am happy because God created me that way, and it doesn't really have to do with the images that I am seeing, which are only symbols or reflections of my joy. Being in a joyful state of mind will automatically bring about spiritual sight because there is nothing to oppose the joy when you are allowing yourself to experience it. Therefore, you will see others as they really are, created by God in joy, innocence, and peace.

When I was observing nature in action in Yellowstone, everything was symbiotic and working in harmony, flowing naturally. Cooperation comes to mind. Cooperation is a reflection of oneness, and a way of joining. The Course is about recognizing that we are all the same, and share the same purpose of awakening in God. Our paths may take different forms, but the content or purpose is the same. When we also work in cooperation with one another, we are essentially saying that we recognize we are joined in a common goal. This is also part of what it means to live a happy dream. In the happy dream, we begin to see with spiritual sight through the forgiveness of our projections, and remembering our brothers are one with us, and that we are all one in God. We've never left our true home. This is what it means to be truly happy.

I have a t-shirt that says, "Vision needs no eyes to see." This is the truth. You could be physically blind and still "see" truly, as Christ, which is really about how you think. That's what matters. Helen Keller, the author, political activist, and lecturer who was also blind and deaf, was a visionary. I have no doubt she was using her third eye and third ear to help her communicate with others. She said, "The only thing worse than being blind is having sight but no vision." She was an example of one who overcame her obstacles and inspired many others to do the same. Mark Twain also said something that represents a similar idea, "The man who doesn't read good books has no advantage over the man who can't read them."

Often times we fear other people because we don't see them truly. I read an anonymous quote, "Fear doesn't stop death; it stops life." That is so true. It reminds me of another quote in the Course that says, *The world is not left by death, but by truth, and truth can be known by all those for whom the Kingdom was created, and for whom it waits.*[8] This passage in the Course can be applied to those moments when we feel sad, depressed, lonely or anxious. There are times when nearly everyone feels defeated in life, and maybe even weary about continuing our journey. When those times come, try and remember the line above, which expresses so clearly the idea that we escape the dream world by practicing true forgiveness, which leads to truth. Death is not an escape, but remembering ourselves as God created us is the way out; remembering true life and that we can live the reflection of that life while still appearing in the world. That is what leads us home.

I remember when I saw a homeless man around our neighborhood, and I knew I was reacting to the image of the man with my ego, because I felt sad. This is not seeing with spiritual sight. It doesn't mean you can't be helpful in some way if you are guided, but I recognized my reaction very quickly and then changed my mind quickly to reflect the Holy Spirit's interpretation. This means that I started thinking about the man as a Son of God, exactly as God created him, perfect spirit, whole and innocent. I reminded myself that this was *my* dream, and so it was my responsibility to see the images I made in my dream correctly. After I did this, I felt guided to go inside my house and get him a blanket because it was cold outside. That was just an effect of my being in my right mind, which took the form of my wanting to be truly helpful in that way. I knew that thinking about him with correct perception was also truly helpful, but sometimes we can be guided to do something or take physical action as well. In this case, that was my inspiration as an act of kindness. I did forgive myself for my projected image of seeing him as a body that can be hurt and afraid. Also, I recognized that I was also afraid in my initial reaction to him, or else I wouldn't have been sad. **So, we are the same. That is the point. To repeat, we all have a wrong mind, right mind, and a decision-maker that chooses between the two.**

When you are seeing someone with spiritual sight, you are doing them and yourself a huge favor. You are sending a message that they are exactly as God created them, not as you made them up. I was seeing this homeless man as I made him, not how he really is in truth. This is especially useful when you are in the presence of someone who is sick. See them as whole, innocent, and nothing less than God. This is how I would want people to see me. You can still be compassionate and kind, and helpful in form, but in your mind you know the truth. *When you meet anyone, remember it is a holy encounter. As you see him you will see yourself. As you treat him you will treat yourself. As you think of him you will think of yourself. Never forget this, for in him you will find yourself or lose yourself.*[9] What you find is your Christ Self as you see the Christ in another. Or, you can join in someone's dream of pain and lose yourself in the body being your identity, which is like being in prison.

There may be times in your life when you feel things are going really well. Just when you thought you were "out of the woods" with forgiveness lessons, then BOOM! Something comes up and you find yourself feeling really bad about something. This is normal along the path of undoing the ego. What's happening is more unconscious guilt is coming to the surface, which is an opportunity to forgive.

In the Development of Trust section in the Course, where Jesus talks about the stages of undoing the ego that we all go through, he reminds us that it's tempting to think that we are farther along on the path than we actually are, but also that we can be further along, but think we are retreating. This is the stage where he describes a period of time when things seem to be a little more peaceful. He says,

> *Now comes "a period of settling down". This is a quiet time, in which the teacher of God rests a while in reasonable peace. Now he consolidates his learning. Now he begins to see the transfer value of what he has learned. Its potential is literally staggering, and the teacher of God is now at the point in his progress at which he sees in it his whole way out. "Give up what you do not want, and keep what you do." How simple is the obvious! And how easy to do! The teacher of God needs this period of respite. He has not yet come as far as he thinks. Yet when he is ready to go on, he goes with mighty companions beside him. Now he rests a while, and gathers them before going on. He will not go on from here alone.*[10]

What we want to give up is the ego, and keep the Holy Spirit's thought system dominant in our minds. In other words, **be vigilant only for God**. We are still learning at this stage what is valuable and valueless, but now we are more trusting that we have the help of the Holy Spirit, and we are applying the principles of forgiveness to all situations, making them equally applicable to everything we see, including people.

The Miracle

It's important to review and understand what the Course refers to as a miracle, as it ties into seeing with spiritual sight. When one first glances at the Course for the first time, it is easy to assume that the miracle in the title refers to physical miracles. After all, all of us are trained to assume and judge that we know what something means from the start without question. This is part of the problem in which the illusory world of time and space was projected. What is interesting about the Course is that Jesus uses the term miracle to mean something entirely different than we've been taught. The miracle in the Course refers to a shift that happens in the mind, when we choose forgiveness instead of judgment or the Holy Spirit's interpretation instead of the egos.

The purpose of the miracle is to undo the ego, the false sense of self that was made up when we chose the illusion of separation over God's perfect oneness. This false self (the ego) has nothing to do with our reality as the Son of God. Furthermore, when we let our lives serve the Holy Spirit's purpose, our lives then become meaningful as we learn to let go of our judgments, interpretations and grievances, which the Course calls mistakes in perception/thinking. The purpose of the miracle is to reverse our thinking and unlearn these mistakes so that we can begin to chip away at the unconscious guilt in the mind. This guilt is a result of the belief that we have sinned over choosing to be separate from each other and from God. As long as we believe we are here in a world of time and space, we are in need of Atonement/healing.

The miracle facilitates the shift in perception that is necessary for us to undo the ego and re-establish our true identity as the Son of God. The miracle is the recognition that you are dreaming a dream, but its contents are not true. When we perform a miracle we are essentially saying that we recognize that what our bodies' eyes are showing us isn't the truth because the body represents a limit on awareness. The Course says that *Whatever is true is eternal, and cannot change or be changed. Spirit is therefore unalterable because it is already perfect, but the mind can elect what it chooses to serve.*[11] Even though truth is eternal and can't be changed, we can choose to forget this. This doesn't change reality, which is good news!

Awakening to our reality as perfect Spirit is a process. It takes time, patience and practice to undo the ego. The more devoted we become to practicing every step we are given along the way, the more results we will experience. Part of the process is that we have to want it! We must want the peace of God above all else. We demonstrate we want it by applying these principles in our everyday lives, bringing our illusions to the truth, and staying vigilant *only* for God (which I will elaborate on more in the last chapter). This is not always an easy process because the ego represents the complete opposite of reality. The ego doesn't want to wake up. Choosing the miracle is threatening to the ego because it means the end of its existence.

Practicing the miracle means to apply true forgiveness to those things that seem to upset us, or those things or people that we think are the cause of our loss of peace. True forgiveness (which is the miracle) places us at cause and not effect. We recognize that we are the dreamers of the dream and therefore can change our mind about the dream. If there is nothing outside the mind, that means that the imagined guilt and fear is in our mind and not out there in the world. The world is an outside picture of what is inside our minds.

My experience of the miracle, having practiced it over and over again for many years, has produced noticeable shifts in my awareness and enhanced my life experience. The form the benefits take for me is that I am less agitated by things that used to bother me, and I am more consistently in a state of peace. Another benefit is that I don't stay upset or agitated as long as before. If I lose my peace of mind, I get back on track much quicker than I used to. This all comes with lots of practice and trust in the process. You may not always see physical results, but that doesn't matter. Forgiveness contributes to the healing of the one mind, regardless if you see results or not. It is worth doing. A peaceful mind brings wonderful gifts! Living the miracle means practicing miracle-minded thinking daily. Eventually, you will notice that you are forgiving automatically instead of judging automatically, and you are becoming more right-minded, which results in experiencing the happy dream. It is worth it. Sometimes, what we think of as "physical miracles" happen, but those are really a symbol or reflection of our spiritual state of abundance. Of course, if we do experience this type of miracle, it's okay to appreciate it. In our minds, we can know what the "real" miracle means.

We all want to be peaceful and experience the joy of God. We all want to feel truly abundant in Him. In the True Prayer exercise I do each day, I like to say, "God, I **have** everything because you **are** everything. You created me as a perfect creation, and I am filled with gratitude that our Will is one." I often joke to myself that I will stop snoozing and start choosing!

It's important to have a spiritual thought system you can be consistent with, regardless of the form it takes. The Course is one path to God, and there are many others. I like the Course because it answers all the questions I have ever had about anything, and also gives us a way through and out of the dream. It's good to recognize what you resonate with, and trust it. Some of you may not resonate with the Course as your chosen path, but if you are new to the Course, and reading the words in this book with a twinge of excitement, it's probably for you. Many people, who find the Course and choose it as a path, have probably studied similar ideas in other lifetimes. You may have walked with Jesus 2000 years ago, following him around trying to figure out what he was saying, like many of us did. I recognized the wisdom in the Course immediately, and sensed that it couldn't have come from this world. It is too sophisticated and consistent for someone in our world to write it on their own. I give credit to Helen Schucman, the scribe of the Course, for taking the seven years it took to take down the notes and finally get it published, with the help of Judith Skutch Whitson, the original publisher of the Course, by *The Foundation for Inner Peace*.

Just for clarification, the following reflects my own personal view about the accuracy of the version of the Course published by *The Foundation for Inner Peace*. This is the version of the Course that was intended for publication according to the direction of Jesus, who assisted Helen (and Bill Thetford – and later, Ken Wapnick) in the final editing of the Course. They were told by Jesus to take out some things (mainly in the first five chapters) that weren't meant for the public, which would have only confused students. Also, Helen's scribing wasn't totally consistent at the beginning, as she was getting used to the style and information in the way Jesus was presenting it. *The Foundation for Inner Peace* is the version that Gary and I use, as well as the one Arten and Pursah quote from. There is no judgment about the other versions that are out there or the people that re-published them. However, as an author myself, I would always appreciate it if others didn't take my work and re-publish it in another form without my permission, which is what happened with the Course. So, the issue is about integrity and keeping with the scribe's guidance (from Jesus) to study the version of the Course from *The Foundation for Inner Peace*.

There has been much controversy around these other versions of the Course, and I have always found in the end, it's better to focus on the content of the message itself rather than the swirling thunder around versions. It doesn't mean I won't give my opinion, but I will always do that without judgment, while at the same time focusing on the true message of the Course itself, which again, is purely non-dualistic.

Jesus says the following about controversy when he is talking about His Course:

All terms are potentially controversial, and those who seek contro-versy will find it. Yet those who seek clarification will find it as well. They must, however, be willing to overlook controversy, rec-ognizing that it is a defense against truth in the form of a delaying maneuver. Theological considerations as such are necessarily con-troversial, since they depend on belief and can therefore be accepted or rejected. A universal theology is impossible, but a universal experience is not only possible but necessary. It is this experience toward which the course is directed.[12]

So, in the end, it's more about applying the principles as they are given, practicing in your everyday life, which brings about an experience of truth. Even in the Workbook of the Course, Jesus says that we may find the ideas hard to believe, but he is asking us to *use* the ideas, not to judge them. We will see that it works if we trust Him. The Workbook is training us to see with spiritual sight, but more specifically, helping us undo the false perception of how we are seeing ourselves and the world now, so that we can start seeing with the true perception of the Holy Spirit. Remember, you may find yourself resisting the exercises, but try not to let that discourage you. The ego mind is very used to a certain set of principles it adheres to very strictly. It's normal to have some trepidation at first. It will pass as you learn to trust in the Holy Spirit.

You may find, as I do, that it's fun to know the truth, and to practice it with everyone and everything in your life that disturbs your peace. As I mentioned earlier in another chapter, life is like a game you play where you know the goal is to forgive and go home. You don't need to rush through it, which only makes it more real. Just take each thing as it comes, focusing on what is right in front of your face on any given day. The lessons are right in front of us to use as opportunities to choose again our reality as Christ. These lessons are the gifts that will return us to the awareness of love's presence when we let go and let God flow through us.

It is a very sneaky trick of the ego to try and change love into something it's not. Instead of letting love be itself, we keep trying to change it. Love doesn't change, and can never change to be something it's not. If we find ourselves wanting to change it, we need to recognize when that is happening, and to forgive ourselves. The formula the Course uses to attain true peace is true forgiveness. **Remember, where there is judgment, there is conflict. Letting go of judgment through forgiveness reduces conflict**. If we all did this every day, we would see a different world. More accurately, we would *experience* a different world.

In summary, spiritual sight is how you are *thinking* about people and the world, not what your body's eyes are showing you. When you are in your right mind as a starting point, you will experience people and the world with love. When you are in your wrong mind as a starting point, you will experience people and the world with conflict. Awareness of this will keep you free from guilt, and in a peaceful frame of mind, which will guide all your actions toward the journey home to God.

Page for Personal Notes

CHAPTER 8

BEYOND THE BODY

Beyond the body, beyond the sun and stars, past everything you see and yet somehow familiar, is an arc of golden light that stretches as you look into a great and shining circle. And all the circle fills with light before your eyes. The edges of the circle disappear, and what is in it is no longer contained at all. The light expands and covers everything, extending to infinity forever shining and with no break or limit anywhere. Within it everything is joined in perfect continuity. Nor is it possible to imagine that anything could be outside, for there is nowhere that this light is not. [1]

I'll never forget the first song I ever wrote at 18 years of age called "The Gift of Love." The first line in the chorus was "The gift of love is all you have to hold onto to make it through this game of life." I was on to something even though I didn't consciously think of life as an illusion just yet. I did catch on it was like a game. In fact, it may be helpful to think of life quite like a game you are playing that comes with instructions on how to play, with a strategy, and even how to end the game successfully.

I came up with some instructions on how to play inspired by Course principles:

The object of the game is to think of life itself as a game, and to forgive as many people as you can and go home. There will be people that will tempt you to judge. When you do, you delay your progress. In order to succeed at the game, you must remember that the people you see aren't really there. They may distract you and suck you into the game even more. The goal is to forgive them regardless of how they act. The more you forgive puts you ahead in the game. You may skip chunks of time, or parts in the game without ever knowing it that get you further along the path. Don't dwell on that, just focus on forgiving. People may hate you, not accept you or may even viciously act out. The hardest part of the game is to remember they are calling for love, and to not dwell on their errors or faults so you can forgive and get closer to home. Any obstacles you may face, such as a physical challenge, financial hardship, or health and relationship problems is part of the game. Again, your job is to remember it's not real so you can forgive and go home. When you come to a point in the game where you have to choose or make a decision, you can choose either the Holy Spirit or the ego as your teacher. One will further root you in the game, and the other will further you on the path to finishing the game. The key to making it through the game in peace is to not judge the game itself or its players, including yourself. The players are playing the game just like you although they don't know it. This may make it more challenging, but if you remember it's only a game, then you will go home and remind them they can go home, too. The best part is when the game is over it will disappear, and you won't even remember you played it. You will only know the truth of your being as it always was; perfect love. There will be no memory of pain or fear, no separate people walking around alone and lonely. There will be nothing more to do…only to be; to be as God created you, in His Holiness. That is the essence of your being.

The Importance of Laughter

Whenever something comes up that seems very serious, I am normal and appropriate with the person or situation, but in my mind I remember to keep a gentle smile and laugh, which helps by watching funny movies. I try not to take myself too seriously. **Laughter is like a fast pass home, along with forgiveness.** Even if a problem or symptoms of something still persist, when you forgive and laugh, you are making progress. I might add that you are not laughing at a person or making fun of them, but you are laughing at the thought that you could be separate from God. That is impossible.

I wrote an article for the Miracle Network on this topic, and I'd like to share it with you now:

"One day I was sitting on my couch feeling very stressed from the seriousness of the day in all its intensity. I could feel my body and muscles tighten up and a deep pressure in my chest. I was alone that night except for my cat, Luna, who was close by, watching me intently. All of a sudden, I exploded with laughter! I was having one of those belly laughs that are unstoppable, just a total giggle fit! There wasn't even a clear reason for the laughter as I wasn't really thinking of anything funny, which made it even funnier. I must have laughed for at least five minutes straight. Tears were rolling down my face I was laughing so hard. Luna was very intrigued and just stared at me like I was crazy. That made me laugh even harder. Then, I found myself laughing out loud these words, 'Everything is so serious! It's so funny! We're all trying so hard to make things work here, to do the right thing, to get our bodies to function, to be successful, to defend ourselves!' The laughter continued for another five minutes. I was laughing at all the seriousness of my ego, but it felt like a really good cleanse for my soul, or a really good workout session. I felt great! Luna kept staring at me and then finally relaxed as if to say, 'Whatever mommy, just get it all out.' I remember thinking when it finally subsided, 'Wow, I feel like I just had a healing session!'

*I think most of us have heard the expression "Laughter is the best medicine." There must be a reason that so many of us seem to agree with this statement. My experience with laughter, especially a good belly laugh, is that it is a release from fear and intensity; a letting go of seriousness. And letting go of seriousness is healing. A Course in Miracles, the non-dualistic thought system which teaches that love and forgiveness are the way home to God, puts laughter in this context: **Into eternity where all is one, there crept a tiny, mad idea at which the Son of God remembered not to laugh.***

In his forgetting did the thought become a serious idea, and possible of both accomplishment and real effects. Together, we can laugh them both away, and understand that time cannot intrude upon eternity. It is a joke to think that time can come to circumvent eternity, which means there is no time.[2]

The Course reminds us that the world was made as an attack on God, which is really a projection of attack coming from the part of the split mind (the ego) that believes it separated from God's love, and then the ego projected the thought that God is now angry at us and is going to punish us for our "sin." Can you say, insane? We actually believed that we could make up a world on our own that is apart from God. Instead of just laughing at the thought that we could oppose God's Will, we made up another world in its place where laughter could not be found. The world we see now has become the world that we believe in. The key word here is belief. A belief doesn't imply knowledge. Knowledge is just known, not believed. We will all come to accept true knowledge, which is of God once we finally let go of the ego all together and accept the correction for the ego, which is what the Course calls the Atonement Principle; the acceptance that nothing happened and the separation from God hasn't occurred. The Course teaches that this is accomplished through true Forgiveness.

Edgar Cayce, the famous "sleeping prophet," also said about laughter, "Laugh in the most extreme circumstance." It seems that well known prophets have emphasized laughter as a necessary part in the process of healing, and awakening from the dream of separation. I think a lot of us take the world and our personal lives so seriously, and this seriousness is what makes the world real. We make it real by our belief in it, as well as the belief that our bodies are who we are. It is in the undoing of the ego and remembering to laugh that we are healed. Fear cannot be seen when laughter is present. Just as the Course says, **If God is real, there is no pain. If pain is real, there is no God.**[3]

It is important to remember not to laugh at another's expense, but only at the silliness of the ego thought system and all of its *childish games. We are being asked in the Course to be childlike, not childish. Jesus is teaching us to maintain our sense of wonder and innocence and become as little children. He says in his brilliant Course, **Little children recognize that they do not understand what they perceive, and so they ask what it means. Do not make the mistake of believing that you understand what you perceive, for its meaning is lost to you.**[4]*

What laughter does is bring us back to that child-like nature and reminds us of our total innocence as God's Son. Every moment we forget to laugh in the face of challenges, we are basically reliving the separation all over again. We are being taught in the Course that we always have a choice as to how we are thinking about ourselves, other people, and the world. Mind is the mechanism of change, and it is the Mind that is at cause. The world is the effect. When we remember to laugh and not take ourselves too seriously, we are essentially choosing to be in our right minds. It always comes down to the choice for innocence or guilt. Whatever we choose is what we believe we are.

Another key point to remember is that all minds are joined. So, when we are in our right minds and in a state of Joy, we are remembering for the whole Sonship. When one heals, we all heal. Laughter says to the unconscious mind, the separation from God has not occurred, we are still whole and innocent, and all is forgiven and released. Seriousness says, the separation from God has really occurred and pain is real. It is always our choice which teacher in our minds we are choosing, the ego or the Holy Spirit. It is this power to choose peace, wholeness, innocence and love reflected in our laughter, that the ego is undone. Then the day will finally come when there is no more need to mentally review dreams. And we will laugh the world away, and live as one forever in God. God Is."

Speaking of laughter, here is another joke for you:

During an impassioned sermon about death and final judgement, the pastor said forcefully, "Each member of this church is going to die and face judgement." Glancing down at the front pew, he noticed a man with a big smile on his face. The minister repeated his point louder. "Each member of this church is going to die and face judgement!" The man nodded and smiled even more. This really got the preacher wound up. He pounded the pulpit emphatically when he came to the ulti-matum: "Each member of this church is going to die and face judge-ment!!!" Though everyone else in the congregation was looking somber, the man in front continued to smile. Finally the preacher stepped off the platform, stood in front of the man and shouted, "I said each mem-ber of this church is going to die!" The man grinned from ear to ear. After the service was over, the preacher made a beeline for the man. "I don't get it," the preacher said in frustration. "Whenever I said, 'Each member of this church is going to die,' your smile got bigger. Why?" "I'm not a member of this church," the man replied.

You can trust the Holy Spirit because the Holy Spirit is the best friend you've ever had, since He knows you as you perfect spirit, whole and innocent. Our identities are wrapped up in bodies, and that is why we suffer. We aren't allowing ourselves to perceive ourselves from the perspective of the Holy Spirit. No one is perfect in regard to behavior, and it is silly to believe we have to be perfect here. It is more important that we practice forgiveness with the things that disturb our peace, and recognizing when we are not happy so that we can practice changing our minds about it. The Holy Spirit wouldn't give us any-thing we couldn't handle.

Bashar, an extra-terrestrial channeled by Darryl Anka, said "You can never lack trust, but you can have one hundred percent trust in lack." In other words, we are always trusting in something, so the ques-tion is *where are we putting our faith and trust?* Why not choose to trust the Holy Spirit? The good news is that you never die. Death is only a thought in the mind. It doesn't exist. God created you eternal. When you dream that you die, your mind just keeps on going. You will realize you can't die. What God creates is eternal, whole, and innocent. **Remember, innocence means to be free of the ego's perception**. When all of us as ONE have no more attachment to the body and world, it will disappear. This idea frightens some people, but that is because of our over-identification with the body and world being our reality. There is nothing to miss in perfect oneness. This is not understandable to an ego mind that believes that to be alone means you don't have another person physically with you. When revelation comes to every mind, it will just be understood.

I've always loved the *St. Francis Prayer for Peace* that describes one who is letting their body be used for the Holy Spirit's purpose. Instead of feeding the needs of the ego, the goal is to seek the wisdom of knowing. It goes like this:

> *Lord, make me an instrument of your peace*
> *Where there is hatred, let me sow love*
> *Where there is injury, pardon*
> *Where there is doubt, faith*
> *Where there is despair, hope*
> *Where there is darkness, light*
> *Where there is sadness, joy*
> *O Divine Master,*
> *Grant that I may not so much seek*
> *To be consoled as to console*
> *To be understood as to understand;*
> *To be loved as to love.*
> *For it is in giving that we receive*
> *It is in pardoning that we are pardoned*
> *And it is in dying that we are born to eternal life.*

There is a film called *Brother Sun, Sister Moon* about St. Francis's life. I highly recommend it. Francis was inspired to leave his wealthy lifestyle and decided to give his life over to the church. He ignited new passion for the love of God among thousands of people. His love and kindness towards animals was apparent, something I always loved about him as well. The body didn't seem as important to him, as he was shedding layers of ego, and becoming more identified with his Christ Self.

When we identify with the body, we are identifying with specialness. Everything we do serves the ego. The Holy Spirit knows we do have needs while we appear to be living in a world, and we can trust we will be taken care of. It's only when we let the ego dominate our minds that it becomes a problem. When we trust the Holy Spirit, and do our best to follow our intuition and natural talents in life, we are serving the higher good, which also means serving ourselves in a humble way. In the big picture, it is always helpful to remember that the body in and of itself is not your reality, nor is your personality really the "real" you. You will see what Jesus thought about the body, which he knew to be an illusion, in the statement below.

Jesus's Message of the Resurrection

Dr. Helen Schucman, the scribe of the Course, asked Dr. Kenneth Wapnick the following question: "Do you think there was a physical resurrection?" Kenneth's response was, "Let's ask the Source/Jesus?" Following is Jesus's response to Helen's inquiry of whether or not there was a physical resurrection, and this absolutely astounded me because of its clarity and certainty of purpose. Please allow yourself to take in this beautiful and remarkable statement from the Master, Jesus:

My body disappeared because I had no illusion about it. The last one had gone. It was laid in the tomb, but there was nothing left to bury. It did not disintegrate because the unreal cannot die. It merely became what it always was, and that is what rolling the stone away means. The body disappears and no longer hides what lies behind it. It merely ceases to interfere with vision.

I did assume a human form with human attributes afterwards to speak to those who were to prove the body's worthlessness to the world. This has been much misunderstood. I came to tell them that death is an illusion, and the mind that made the body can make another one since form itself is an illusion.

They didn't understand, but now I talk to you, and I'm going to give you the same message. The death of an illusion doesn't mean anything. It disappears when you awaken and decide to dream no more and the thoughts that create it are gone. And you still do have this power to make the same decision as I did. God or Love holds out His hand to His Son to help him rise and return to Him. I can help because the world is an illusion and I have overcome the world. So, look past the tomb/the body/the illusion. Have faith in nothing but the Spirit and the guidance God gives you.

He could not have created the body because it's a limit. He must have created the Spirit because it's immortal, so can those who were created like Him be limited? The body is the symbol of the world, leave it behind, it cannot enter Heaven, but I can take you there anytime you choose. Together we can watch the world disappear and its symbol vanish, and then I cannot speak of that. A body cannot stay without illusions, and the last one to be overcome is death. That's the message of the crucifixion. There is no order of difficulty in miracles. That's the message of the resurrection. Miracles are those offerings of love. Illusions are illusions; truth is true; illusions vanish; only Truth remains.

These lessons needed to be taught but once, for when the stone of death is rolled away, what can be seen except an empty tomb? And that is what you see who follow me into the sunlight and away from death, past all illusions into Heaven's gate where God will come Himself to take you home.[5]

This story astounds me because Jesus is saying his body disappeared because he had no more illusion about it. He just made or projected another body when he appeared to the disciples. This is an important point because all of us who appear to be here are also projecting our bodies, but we don't think of it that way. When there is no attachment or illusion about the body, there is no cause for it, so it simply ceases to exist. It was never real in the first place. I recommend you re-read Jesus's response several times and really let it sink in.

Beyond the body is life; *real* life. The body obscures what lies beyond it because that is the ego's purpose for the body; to hide the truth of your reality. The body is a limit, but your reality is unlimited. Beyond the body is wholeness, oneness, perfection; God. It is abstract with no bodies or limits. Love extends into eternity. This is what we are awakening to. This is Heaven.

There is no hell, only a belief in hell. Hell is merely separation, and Heaven is oneness. If there is no hell, then there can be no devil. The devil only means *that which is not good for you.* Evil can be translated to mean *ego viciously ignoring love.* **Remember, there are only calls for love and expressions of love.** Are you starting to think in pure non-dualistic terms? Pure non-dualism means there is *only* God/Love, which is the only reality.

Being the Observer of Your Dream

In my private sessions with people, I often have people be the observer of their problems from above the battleground, which means you look with Jesus or the Holy Spirit (same thing) at your life without judgment. There is a way to remain in a neutral state no matter what is happening around you. This means that you observe yourself and the figures in your dream without attachment to any particular outcome. This may be the hardest part, even with forgiveness: Letting go of attachment to outcomes. Remember, we don't know and can't see what is best for everyone, but the Holy Spirit can. All we need to do is let love be itself through us, and get out of our own way. We need to be aware of and remove the blocks to love. Those blocks are our attack thoughts that we have about ourselves or other people. Attack thoughts come from the belief we are guilty for separating from God. So, you can see that ultimately it's the guilt in our minds that is running the ego's show, but looking at the guilt with the Holy Spirit, we would see that there is no cause for it because the separation from God never happened. As you progress through the Course, this idea becomes more and more apparent.

In practice, this is done when we don't react to other people's errors with our egos. It doesn't mean we don't respond, but the response would come from love, not fear or anger. When we don't react, we are essentially saying that the person's behavior has had no effect on us. When there is no effect, there can be no cause (of something outside of us to make us upset). Do you see? This demonstrates to the other person that their mistake is not a cause for guilt. This will plant a seed to help the other person choose the same mindset when he/she is ready. At the same time, you are reinforcing this powerful idea in your own mind, that what you are cannot be hurt. When Jesus talked about *turning the other cheek*, he wasn't saying that we should ignore the other person because they are an illusion. He was saying that we can demonstrate to the other person that what we all are in truth (the Son of God as one) cannot be hurt because we are not bodies. Remember the re-interpretation of the crucifixion in Chapter 7? That is the idea or mindset one can have, which brings true freedom from pain in any form. It is important to remember that until you get very good at this mindset, which requires training, there will be times when you still get upset. Try not to judge yourself for this, just forgive.

There are many times in life when it's difficult to perceive yourself in any other way than in a body. This can be especially difficult when you are feeling pain in the body. To be beyond the body is how you are thinking about it, not that you have to literally try and get out of your body. In fact, the body is in your mind, so you can practice changing your mind about it. Sometimes the pain will go away and sometimes it may not. The point is that there is always something there to learn if the willingness is there to learn it. I've had my share of physical issues so I can speak with some experience. It's not always easy, but truly possible to weaken the ability of the ego to affect you. In other words, everything is helpful when we are using it for the Holy Spirit's purpose of forgiveness.

In my early 20's, I was having all kinds of interesting experiences of being "out of my body." Even though we never really go "out of the body" since the body is in the mind, we can certainly have the experience that we do, which is called an "out of body experience." Also, being "out of the body" is not the same thing as being "beyond the body," as referred to in the Course. Beyond the body means that we recognize we are in the Mind of God, observing our dream of being a body with the Holy Spirit as our teacher.

The mind is always making images, but these images are not our reality. When we dream, whether it's the daytime or night-time dreams, there will always be duality, because that is the nature of dreams. It's not perfect oneness. Whenever we are experiencing frightening images, we can remember that the light of the Holy Spirit is stronger than any darkness we dream of.

To make a point, I remember one afternoon in the mid 90's when I was feeling vulnerable and tired after having been sick with the flu. I fell asleep and had a dream of a ghostly figure in a vast field, and the figure started flying towards me at a very high speed. This was very concerning to me in the dream because it looked like it wasn't going to stop at my body. As soon as it reached my body, I woke up and opened my eyes, and I felt this energy still in my body, and it felt as though it was trying to get me to jump outside my own window, which was 5 stories up from the ground. I absolutely did not want to go. I said with conviction, "I don't want to go, I don't want to go!" My will was very strong. It felt like a brief possession of a spirit. Finally, it felt like it left me, and I remained there on the bed, but paralyzed for a few minutes. I couldn't move one muscle. I tried, but couldn't do it.

I have had similar experiences with being paralyzed while awakening from a dream, and I later learned that it's a common experience for those that often have "Out of body experiences." The experience I described above seemed a little different, more like an energetic presence overtook my body for a minute to the point where if I had let go, who knows what would have happened. I share this to show that when your will is strong, and you remember the light of God or the Holy Spirit, that is way more powerful than the darkness. It's like when you switch on a light in the room, it is no longer dark. Same thing when you think of the Holy Spirit. It shines away any dark thoughts. I am a very vivid dreamer, and I remember my dreams to the point where it sometimes becomes hard to tell the difference between which is the night-time and day-time dream. It's that real. At the same time, *none* of it's real. Whenever I have a nightmare, I remember this from the Course: *The images you make cannot prevail against what God Himself would have you be.*[6] This always brings peace to my mind. Lately, I have noticed that whenever I have a nightmare, which is rare these days, I am able to shrug it off as soon as I remember the truth.

I am an advocate of paying attention to your dreams, because they can often be prophetic. The Holy Spirit will speak to you in your dreams if you ask to be given information, and remain open and willing to receive without any expectation of outcomes. Beings often communicate to me in my dream state, and I can tell the difference now if it's a mischievous energy or a genuine light being. The point is that you can use your dreams to your benefit if you are open. It can even be fun! I always remember first thing in the morning that I am just awakening to another dream, so I am not tempted to make any of it real. On the level of the world, there are certainly beings that are open to communication with us, including extra-terrestrials. For those that are interested, we have to match their vibration in order to see or hear them. These beings will communicate more with us as time goes on when the windows of opportunity present themselves. Most often, they will appear in your dreams as a gentler way of introducing themselves.

I bring up these stories because even though the world is an illusion, and we are not really our bodies, as long as we appear here we might as well enjoy the ride, and all of the interesting sights we will see along the journey. The key is enjoying the journey without attachment or investment in the dream being the cause of anything. It's only an effect of thought. The dream and its figures aren't the cause of your happiness or sadness. Mind is cause, the world is the effect. As one progresses through the Course and becomes more advanced in its principles, the experience the Course is directed towards is felt with more intensity. The love we forgot has not forgotten us. Jesus encourages us to recognize that when we see through the bodies eyes we aren't really seeing, so we are all spiritually blind through the device of separation. We lack true vision.

The quote above at the beginning of this chapter is from a beautiful section in the Course called "The Forgotten Song." This passage is describing to us the world of non-dualistic knowledge, inspiring us to expand our minds beyond form. The song refers to the oneness of Heaven's love. This is what we forgot, but will remember with the Holy Spirit's help. There are no concepts in Heaven including an outside or inside, as the outside is just a projection of what is within. Yet even the idea of "within" is meaningless when it is recognized that there is only the awareness of perfect oneness in Heaven.

Some of the passages in "The Forgotten Song" can be used as a beautiful meditation. I would suggest you record it in your own voice, and play it back to yourself. It is a complete picture of the oneness between the Father and Son. I like to think of this oneness as a dance the Father and Son have with each other. The Father moves first, and then the Son responds in a similar fashion, dancing in harmony with no break or limit in the music. We know this dance well, but it is blocked from our awareness, just as the clouds obscure the sun, although the sun still shines.

As a result of undoing the ego and the mind opening, you may experience things that seem unfamiliar to you at first, such as more psychic awareness, or light around objects. Your dreams may become more vivid, and even cross over to the point where you have to think which dream was night-time and which was daytime. There is nothing to be afraid of when this happens. Your mind is awakening and you are beginning to see that you are a mind and not a body. In fact, life can even be more fun with this awareness because you don't have to take everything so seriously. Your only goal becomes to be truly helpful. The ego may try and fight you, and it may seem sometimes that things are getting worse before they get better. This is because the ego is sensing a threat to its existence. The Course is asking us to look at the ego or darkness because we've made it real, so we need to look at it before we can move beyond it, beyond the body to the light of God. The dark thoughts in our minds were always there, but now we are noticing them more so we can forgive them, which removes more unconscious guilt from our minds. This is why people say things like, "Everything was fine until I started doing the Course. Things are getting worse for me." It's not that things are really getting worse. The attack thoughts were always there. Again, it's because the Course is asking us to look more closely at the thoughts we've been choosing which are not making us happy, so that we can choose the Holy Spirit's perception instead of the ego, which does make us truly happy.

There are no limits to a mind that knows its reality is God. This unlimited nature of the mind can be reflected in the dream through the ability to do all kinds of cool things, like time travel, mind transport, astral travel, healing oneself of illnesses, and much more. The best use of mind would be to use it to shift our thinking to reflect love instead of fear; innocence instead of guilt. It doesn't mean we can't have fun in the dream if we do it responsibly.

I'll never forget an experience I had almost 20 years ago while I was in between the sleeping and awake state. I was lying in my bed, and I started to have an out of body experience. I saw my ethereal or astral arms lift out of myself, and my upper body started to follow and lift up and out. For some reason I hesitated, and my ethereal arms floated back down into my body's arms, like a hand fitting into a glove. Then, I looked up and saw a transparent, round sphere of light floating about seven feet above me. I wasn't afraid, just curious. It looked kind of like a large, clear bubble, maybe with a blue tint to it. I thought to myself that maybe it was a guide of mine or some kind of intelligence visiting me. It just stayed there, floating above me for a couple of minutes. I didn't know what to do, so I just observed it. Then, I fell back asleep. Several years later I was having a session with Kevin Ryerson, a medium who was made famous by appearing in Shirley Maclaine's movie, *Out On A Limb,* where he actually gave a live reading to Shirley in the film. I asked the Spirit, Atun-Re, who was speaking through Kevin, about my experience with the sphere of light. He said what I saw was called a Bindu, or Blue Pearl, and that it is a vehicle of transport. I could have entered it like a room, and it could take me anywhere along the timeline. In other words, it's like a way of time traveling. Wow! I was so annoyed that I didn't know that at the time. Maybe I wouldn't have been ready for that. I've never seen it since, but at least I would know what is possible if I do see it again. I started to think of where I would want to go (the illusory past or future). I thought it would be cool to observe what it was like during the lifetime I had as Thaddeus, a disciple of Jesus. Or, perhaps go 500-1000 years into the future to see what the world would be like. Even though the idea of time travel is a cool one, I always remember that time is not linear, but happening all at once. That is why time travel is actually possible. In Egyptian art, there are often blue spheres surrounding figures as if they are in some kind of vehicle of transport. I believe this is what I saw. I do like to have fun, and I love adventure, so exploring other dimensions of time and even other civilizations besides those on earth have always been exciting to me. That just means they are part of my script, and there is a reason for it.

Remember, it's okay to have hobbies, and pursue what excites you. In fact, since we have a choice, why wouldn't we do that? We all have preferences, and it makes sense to follow them. At the end of the day, I remember it's all a dream, whether it's night-time, daytime, or even meeting other beings on other planets. This helps me to not be attached to the world as my true home.

Something to think about that will help you to apply forgiveness is that things may still come up that you would define as negative. Forgiveness doesn't mean that things in the world or in your own life will always be pleasant. It means to be in the midst of those things and still be at peace. I love the Serenity Prayer, which was written by the American theologian Reinhold Niebuhr (1892–1971). It goes like this:

God, grant me the serenity to accept the things I cannot change,
Courage to change the things I can,
and wisdom to know the difference.

The things we can't change are the world and other people; the script in general. What we *can* change is our minds *about* the world. As we continue to practice, we will learn to discern the difference between the two. We change the world by concentrating on our own forgiveness lessons, not somebody else's. It's very tempting to want to change other people. What we want to change in other people is really a reflection of what we need to change within ourselves. When you think about other people's behavior and there is something you don't like, that "something" you don't like wouldn't bother you if you didn't first identify with a similar quality in yourself. Otherwise, you would just be at peace. Coming back to spiritual sight, the correction for this is to look at the content in your mind and remember that you can change your mind about what you are thinking. **You don't have to agree with people, but you can forgive them using the steps of true forgiveness outlined in this book.**

Think what beyond the body really means. Then, you can use the tools given to take things step by step to work your way up the ladder to the real world. The real world, where all is forgiven, is a process over time, or a lifetime of practice. **Watch for the tricks of the ego that tell you that you need to be further along on the path, or that you are not doing it right, or that everything in your life should be going well all the time. It doesn't work that way**. What happens is that your mind is becoming more peaceful along the way, so that no matter what happens you are in a miraculous frame of mind; a forgiving mind. You may want to try practicing letting go of the need to control the outcomes to things. This can be hard sometimes, but worth the practice. When you are doing something, do it for the enjoyment of it, not for what it will produce for you, which is an expectation of an outcome. Whenever we are following what naturally brings us the most excitement at every given moment, we are in the flow of life, and life will flow through you and guide you in the most synchronistic way.

In my experience, I have found this to be absolutely true. As soon as I surrender the need to control outcomes, and just follow my guidance in every moment, things are much more synchronistic. Being naturally excited about things without the investment in outcomes is your intuition speaking to you; listen to it carefully. It will help you stay in the flow of life.

In summary, let love teach you of itself, which is learning about your true Self through open-mindedness, forgiveness, honesty, patience, and letting go of the temptation to change love into something it's not. The Course is not a course on love. It's a course on removing all the blocks to the awareness of love, which is our natural state. To be beyond the body is to recognize that you are mind, and there is nothing outside of you. This is what we are learning. As long as we are dreaming we are in a body, it can be used lovingly, which means we can use it to heal our illusions of separation, and return home to God.

Page for Personal Notes

CHAPTER 9

THE BUSINESS OF FORGIVENESS

*Forgiveness is the only thing that stands for truth in the illusions
of the world. It sees their nothingness, and looks straight through
the thousand forms in which they may appear. It looks on lies,
but it is not deceived. It does not heed the self-accusing shrieks
of sinners mad with guilt. It looks on them with quiet eyes, and
merely says to them, "My brother, what you think is not the truth."* [1]

*One day the Buddha was teaching, and a high Priest in the Hindu culture
became angry at what he was teaching, and confronted him while he was
meditating. He projected many abuses on him, and the Buddha just sat
there and smiled. The Priest became aware that the Buddha was just sitting
there, and he said, "Aren't you angry that I have laid so many abuses on
you?" The Buddha said, "No, you came and you spoke any number of different abuses, however, I have not accepted any of those abuses, so therefore
in my not receiving them they had nowhere to go except to return to their
source. But I don't want you to feel any abuses either, so there is really no
need to be angry."*

The above story is an example of a forgiving mind. When someone
lays an abusive thought, word, or deed on you, and you don't accept it
as yours, it can't hurt you. There is nowhere for that energy to go except
back to the person that projected it. If someone lays an abuse on you,
and there is already a belief in your mind that you are unworthy, then it

will feel hurtful. So the key is to heal the limiting beliefs we have about ourselves through forgiveness so that we can be free of suffering.

When we choose to hold on to grievances, we are anchoring ourselves to a past that doesn't exist. Forgiveness helps us lift that anchor to the past so that we can be free in the present, which is truly being as God created you. Others also have their own path, and you don't have to make their path your business. Make forgiveness your business, always. Also, you can use any disturbance you experience to re-define what it means for you. Expand your definitions so that they support you in your awareness as perfect Spirit, whole and innocent, not further root you in dreams.

Whenever someone asks me what business I'm in, I always answer normally, but in my mind I know I'm in the business of forgiveness. Actually, in my profession it is quite accurate to say that! Afterall, I do teach the Course, which is truly being in the business of forgiveness. The good news is that anyone can choose to make forgiveness your business no matter what your cover job is here in the world. Speaking of that, the jobs we do in the world aren't as important as *how* and with *whom* we do it. When we turn our jobs over to the Holy Spirit, it's serving a holy purpose. Just because the world is an illusion, it doesn't mean you have to stop your job or even change jobs. Just do as you're trained and let it serve the Holy Spirit, and you will be truly helpful to others. For example, if you are an energy healer, just because energy is mis-created thought, or part of the illusion, doesn't mean you should stop being an energy healer. People need different forms of help and guidance. It's not always so black and white when it comes to the world. Sacrifice is unnecessary, so you don't have to give anything up, unless you truly feel you are ready to move on. Anytime you feel you need to give up something in the dream from the perspective of it's not spiritual enough, it is making it real. So, it's nice to know we can be ourselves and follow our natural talents in the dream. We get lots of questions about this. There is a reason you are drawn to the field you are in. It's part of your script. You may also be learning lessons, such as learning how to be at peace in your job and forgiving relationships with co-workers. You may be learning that you can find solutions that create win-win situations for everyone involved. I don't know any job that is 100 percent perfect all the time. **The goal is not to have the perfect job, life, relationship, body, etc. It's to be in peace no matter what. That is possible.**

Being Vigilant Only For God

When you know that forgiving anything that comes up on any given day is your real job, it takes some pressure off to be perfect in the world. The idea is: When we're always trying to fix the screen, or change other people/the outer picture, that intervention we are always hoping someone else will get, is really for us. We need to intervene in our own minds where the cause is. But sometimes it's harder to do in certain situations, and it is during these times when the realization hits that the pain comes from our own thinking with the ego and doesn't have to do with anybody else. The pain of recognizing our own inner pain that we project outside of ourselves is something we need to deal with. The pain is always the result of unconscious guilt over the separation. The work is understanding that you are worth the consistent effort to keep building respect for yourself, not having someone else prove they can be respectful to you; to keep seeing yourself in high esteem, with high regard. There is no one else. In building your spiritual house from within, the Holy Spirit will be there and guide you with the steps to take that are in alignment with your inner efforts. Ultimately, the outer picture tends to take care of itself when the inner picture is nurtured. Things fall into place. The final work is to then trust that it is being taken care of and things will be okay. Practice letting go of outcomes and the way you think things should look. Things are always okay, but we don't believe that.

To be vigilant *only* for God and His Kingdom means that we are understanding what is undesirable (thinking with the ego) and what it costs us, so that the choice for the Holy Spirit is obvious, and what would truly make us happy. It is clear that as a human race, we have been vigilant for the ego. Jesus assures us in the Course that…*you can be as vigilant against the ego as for it.*[2] Being vigilant is being consistent in our practice so that it becomes a priority, with no exceptions. This means that despite the chaos that might swirl around you, you are still demonstrating the choice for the right-mind by being a living example of forgiveness. Eventually, there will be no need to choose because you will realize that anything outside the Kingdom of Heaven is not God. This is true freedom, and leads you to extend love as God does, which is creating in the Kingdom.

The Peace of God

I understand when people say things like, "How can I have peace when I am in so much pain?" Or, "My loved one is dying and I have no more family; I have no money; my job is not exciting anymore; I'm out of a job, and I can't pay my bills; the fires, earthquakes, and hurricanes have displaced me and my family. How is peace possible under these conditions?" These can be devastating experiences, and it wouldn't be helpful to deny them. We are not asked to deny our experiences, but we can work on forgiving them. What does that look like in practice? Well, it means that you do the normal thing in the world to get yourself back on track the best you can, ask for help when you can, remembering that it's a sign of strength to ask for help, and then in your mind you practice forgiveness at the same time. In order for peace to come, the world must be looked at differently. In other words, the script is written, and although you can't change that, you can choose how you see it. **The script itself is not personal. In other words, we make it personal by how we react to it. Remember, the Holy Spirit is in charge of whether or not you shift dimensions of time. Let Him handle that part.** Forgiveness offers benefits we can't see. You might shift dimensions of time so that you experience the same event differently. You still see the event and the same people, but your perception shifts so it doesn't bother you. You don't have to be concerned with when or how this happens, just trust that forgiveness leads to all kinds of great things you can't even imagine. Exercising your ability to choose how you perceive something, and without judgment, is a necessary step to returning to a peaceful mind.

I mentioned that the attainment of the peace of God is the goal of the Course. In truth, we already are the peace of God, but the majority of us haven't accepted it yet. This is because the ego's voice is very loud. As you know by now, this voice is an illusion, but the ego doesn't want you to know that. It has drowned out the Voice of the Holy Spirit for the purpose of keeping us mindless and in a state of separation, which is a limitation. These two voices are mutually exclusive. One leads to pain, the other to peace. Whichever one you choose will determine the experience you have. The ego has tricked us into believing that pain equals love. What pain equals is more pain.

In light of the questions I presented above, there is a section in the Course in the *Manuel for Teachers* that asks the question: *How is Peace Possible in This World?*[3] Jesus talks about judgment and says, *In your judgment it is not possible, and can never be possible. But in the Judgment of God what is reflected here is only peace.*[4] *This time ask yourself whether your judgment or the Word of God is more likely to be true. For they say different things about the world, and things so opposite that it is pointless to try to reconcile them.*[5]

In other words, we can't reconcile truth and illusion, ego and Holy Spirit, life and death. It's one or the other, and they can't both be true. Once we make the choice on a consistent basis for truth, peace becomes inevitable. We may believe we have lots of problems, and as I mentioned, as long as we believe we do, we can do our best to resolve them. At the same time, the mindset of the Course leads us to remember that...*the Holy Spirit is the Answer to all problems you have made. These problems are not real, but that is meaningless to those who believe in them. And everyone believes in what he made, for it was made by his believing it.*[6]

These judgments can be corrected by first being aware when you are judging, which you will know by how you feel, then changing your mind about it. Peace comes when we offer peace to others. The world does nothing, and the world is not the cause of our loss of peace. The choice to see a world of pain, opposite to God's love is the problem. **The whole way out is to change the way we see; that is the point.**

Ultimately, the day will come when you are in the "real world," which means you have forgiven the world for what you thought it did to you. You will no longer see the world as attacking you, but will see it as calling out for love. This is when you are truly free, as the blocks to the awareness of love's presence have been removed. You've let go of your grievances and judgments. You will know that everyone is worthy of love because we are all the same, and on the same path home to God. No one will be excluded from this love. Then, words can't speak of what lies beyond. You will just understand. This is the experience of the happy dream!

It's time for a joke, so we don't get too serious about the world:

A mother was preparing pancakes for her boys, Kevin 5, and Ryan 3. The boys began to argue over who would get the first pancake. Their mother saw the opportunity for a moral lesson. "If Jesus were sitting here, he would say, 'Let my brother have the first pancake, I can wait.'" Kevin turned to his younger brother and said, "Ryan, you be Jesus!"

There is no one in this world who doesn't suffer at some point. The good news is that when we understand where suffering comes from, we put ourselves in the position of being at cause so that we can start taking steps toward changing it. Suffering can be corrected in an instant, but usually that is not our experience. When the feeling of suffering is present, it means that there is a belief in our minds that the world has hurt us in some way. To the ego, this is salvation. The ego wants to keep us in a mindless state of being unfairly treated by something "outside" ourselves so that our victimization story continues. This way, we are not accountable for our own thinking. We remain unconscious that we are the dreamers of our dream so that we don't see that all attack is brought upon by ourselves. This makes it impossible to escape the suffering because we have defined the source as being outside ourselves.

The Course gives us a way to escape by helping us see what the "real" problem is instead of how we set it up for ourselves. The Course is teaching us that just as we assume we know what the best outcome is in any situation, we also assume we know what the problem is (of which there seems to be many) so that we set ourselves up for thinking we know the answer to the problem. We define problems on our own and then attempt to solve them on our own. This never works in a way that brings lasting peace. So, let's take a look at what the Course says about problems. Before you read this, please think of all the problems you think you have right now, no matter what the form, just let them come to mind. Then, read the following statement:

A problem cannot be solved if you do not know what it is. Even if it is solved already you will still have the problem, because you will not recognize that it has been solved. This is the situation of the world. The problem of separation, which is really the only problem, has already been solved. Yet the solution is not recognized because the problem is not recognized.[7]

Everyone in this world seems to have his own special problems. Yet they are all the same, and must be recognized as one if the one solution that solves them all is to be accepted. Who can see that a problem has been solved if he thinks the problem is something else? Even if he is given the answer, he cannot see its relevance.[8]

Many of us think of ourselves as having an endless list of problems. When one is solved, it seems as if another arises, and it goes on and on. This is how the ego set it up, so that the problem of separation remains unsolved. You do not have to settle for such a depressing interpretation. When you start to see that all problems have been solved because the separation has been solved, you will see that you cannot fail. This requires acceptance of seeing the problem as it is so that you can choose the correction. Ultimately, when the "real" problem is recognized, you will also see that you have no problems. Why? **Because where there is no self, there are no problems.** This is when peace comes.

The Course asks us to repeat the idea often to ourselves that our only problem has been solved, and to do it with conviction and gratitude. *You are entitled to peace today. A problem that has been resolved cannot trouble you. Only be certain you do not forget that all problems are the same. Their many forms will not deceive you while you remember this. One problem, one solution. Accept the peace this simple statement brings.*[9]

In some cases, you may feel so much resistance that it seems impossible for you to go any further in experiencing peace. When this happens, sit quietly and accept without judgment that this is your experience now, but it doesn't mean that it has to be defined as negative or bad. You can still use it to your advantage if you see it as a classroom for learning. That's all it is. Just allow your feelings in that moment, but ask the Holy Spirit to look at them with you. Be the neutral observer of your thoughts, just looking at them as if you are watching a movie of yourself sitting there thinking. You don't have to take yourself so seriously. This can calm your mind, and re-direct you toward a balanced and right-minded state of mind.

Whenever I get anxious or can't seem to calm my mind, I do the exercise above. I allow my feelings without judging them, and I even say, "So what? This isn't negative or bad unless I define it that way. I can use this to my advantage by seeing it as an opportunity to choose forgiveness and think different thoughts; to remember that I am completely supported by the Holy Spirit." This helps me a lot.

In many places in the Course, we are asked to say things to ourselves with determination and conviction. Jesus knows we doubt ourselves to the point where we get ourselves stuck in an endless cycle. Having willingness to practice and apply His teachings will lead us to the peace of God. In practice, a forgiving mindset can look like this:

Practice letting go of judgment and giving up the idea that you know what is best for you, other people, the country, etc. because we can't know what that is. Things don't look like they make sense in the world. We look at the world and things look "crazy." They don't make sense. This is because it's a dream, and dreams are chaotic since they come from a chaotic thought. **You can transcend the chaos, the thunder and lightning swirling around you, and stay in your calm center, the quiet center, and know that the thunder and lightning swirling around you has nothing to do with you unless you make it your business. It's not your business; forgiveness is.** It's only your business if you take it personally and react as if it were real (with the ego).

When you are in your right mind, you will be helpful no matter what chaos is going on around you in the world. It doesn't mean you deny or ignore the world, but you will be in your right mind, which means you will be truly helpful. That will take the form of whatever is best for everyone. When we are reacting with fear, uncertainty and doubt, anger and attack, which are all forms of judgment, about what the world is doing, we are having moments of insanity because we are reacting to our own projections. We're seeing things that aren't there, and hearing things that aren't there. Remember, we are watching this in our own minds. We are mentally reviewing a chaotic world, but it doesn't have to be chaotic in your mind. Jesus says the images you see can be transformed - and be so lovely when things are being a reflection of the Holy Spirit. The images in and of themselves aren't lovely, but the content of your right mind is being changed, and it becomes lovely because you only see innocence, truth, and Christ. You look past the forms, the errors, the facades/illusions, seeing only truth. The images you see aren't real. Just like in your dreams in bed at night, your day-time images are also made up. It's no different. The Holy Spirit maintains its presence in your mind, always guiding you, and whispering to you and reminding you to look past troubling images, remembering it's only a dream.

You can wake up from this nightmare by having daily moments of forgiveness if you need it, of those things that upset you; daily moments of recognizing you can choose again, which is what forgiveness has us do; daily moments of walking the world and reminding yourself that you are not of the world; daily moments of remembering that you are in Heaven, only dreaming of hell; daily moments of recognizing that all the people you see "out there" aren't really there, rather they are perfect Spirit, whole and innocent, still as one with you at home in God; daily moments of remembering that when you get upset that you are never upset for the reason you think. "When my partner disturbs me; when my co-worker disturbs me 'I am never upset for the reason I think, because they are not the problem. They are not the cause, because the cause is not outside of me, it is in my mind. I am choosing to see it this way.'" This is an attitude you can have every day. It can become so consistent that there is absolutely nothing that can ever threaten you or take away your peace ever again. This is what it means to practice living these ideas in your everyday life.

Awakening is a journey, not something that happens overnight. So we need to be patient and forgive ourselves when we are tempted to judge ourselves for not accepting these truths in an instant. We can forgive ourselves when we have moments when we do feel guilty or angry, or unfairly treated, or when we believe the world is doing something to us. We all have those moments. As long as we are here, we will make mistakes, but it's just a mistake, not a sin. Just like the one Son of God once appeared to wander off from the Father, the Father doesn't pursue him in anger, scolding him and punishing him for running off, but gently notices that His Son has wandered off. He doesn't make it real by reacting to it with anger, which reminds His Child it didn't happen. There is nothing He did wrong, or to be punished for. Does innocently wandering off call for so much vengeance and punishment? All the things we do to each other? Does it require all that pain when we remember that it was just this one little "tiny mad idea?" We are still God's Holy Son, exactly as He created us. He isn't concerned with what we think we did. He just wants us to wake up and come home; home to His perfect love.

A Forgiveness Story

Sometimes forgiveness can take an unexpected turn, where the forgiver ends up working in some way with the person they needed to forgive, which demonstrates the joining of the mind with another in the awareness that we are all working toward a common goal. The following is a true story that was brought to my attention, so I tell the story below as it was related to me:

"There was a woman whose grandson was about to leave the house. He was about 15 or 16 years old, African-American, and had a promising scholarship, etc. He was leaving his grandmother and heading home when he encountered a number of Ku Klux Klan types who beat him to death. In the court proceedings, one of the perpetrators of the crime/of the murder of the grandson had turned state evidence. During the trial, the grandmother was sitting in the front row with other family members, and the perpetrator was giving evidence against his fellow perpetrators when suddenly he turned to the grandmother and said, "What I'm going to ask I know I don't deserve. I'm going to prison and I'm going to get what I deserve. But I can't live with myself unless I have your forgiveness for taking your grandson's life." The African-American woman looked at him and said, "When my grandson left that night, somehow I knew he wouldn't be coming home again. It was at that moment when I knew he wouldn't be coming home that I forgave you."

So even before the act occurred she had already forgiven him. The man went to prison, and every time he came up for parole, the grandmother was there testifying that he should be released because she felt he was no longer the person he had been. Eventually he did have a successful parole and he worked with the grandmother. She took him to his halfway house during his probation period and then they began cooperating together, going around speaking against violence."

The story above demonstrates that not only can a person forgive, but can remain in a positive state in such a way that he/she can even collaborate with the other toward a common goal. This action step isn't required for forgiveness to be effective, but it's an example of what is possible. In this example, the grandmother was clearly not making what happened "real" by holding on to grievances. Instead, she channeled it into a higher purpose. In the highest reality of perfect love, it didn't even happen, since all our time is spent in dreaming. This kind of thinking, however, is an advanced state that requires practice and patience. Having a daily, forgiving attitude is what will lead us all to the experience of our oneness with God.

Lesson 121 in the Course's workbook, *Forgiveness is the key to happiness,*[10] is encouraging us to transcend the specialness of our relationships and see the holiness in all people. In fact, Jesus makes it crystal clear that forgiveness is always the answer to suffering of any kind. He says, *Here is the answer to your search for peace. Here is the key to meaning in a world that seems to make no sense. Here is the way to safety in apparent dangers that appear to threaten you at every turn, and bring uncertainty to all your hopes of ever finding quietness and peace. Here are all questions answered; here the end of all uncertainty ensured at last.*[11]

What could be more reassuring than to be assured we have the answer to all our problems! We just need to let go of what we think our lives are supposed to look like in order for us to be happy. **Happiness is not dependent on anything external. It's an inside job**.

If there is one way to tell if you have truly forgiven something it is this: When you are able to talk or think about a person or situation that used to disturb you in some way, but now you can talk or think about it in a neutral way, without the negative energy attached to it, and with no more expectations of a certain outcome having to play out for you to be happy, it is forgiven. More simply, this can be stated as "I am truly at peace with this." You will know when you are peaceful because there will be no doubt or uncertainty. Also, when you are in a forgiving state of mind, you will experience more synchronicities, and time may seem different to you, or you may feel time has extended for you. Things may seem lighter and dreamier, not so solid. Sometimes I'm walking around and I just stop and observe the scene around me and I actually say to myself, "I'm feeling the dream. This doesn't seem real." It's a pretty interesting feeling walking around like you are on a movie set with backdrops, sound effects, and fancy lights.

Arten and Pursah, the Ascended Master teachers in Gary's books, have said that when they appear to Gary they have just enough feeling to function in a body, but it feels so light to them, since they are aware they are projecting their bodies into the dream. **Note:** Many people have asked me if Arten and Pursah have appeared to me since Arten is my future self in my next incarnation. The answer is no, they have not appeared to me yet. When Gary asked Arten and Pursah if they were ever going to appear to me, they didn't exactly say no. It sounded like they left the idea open, and even stated that part of whether or not they appear to me is up to me. I think I know what they mean. I trust that they will appear to me if it's helpful to do so. They know what's best. Or, maybe it's just not necessary. Either way, I am at peace. Even if they appeared to me, I'd still have my forgiveness lessons! Life goes on. Also, everyone has access to the Holy Spirit, equally. That is their message along with forgiveness.

I do feel inspired by the Holy Spirit in my work and writings, and Arten and Pursah are really the Holy Spirit showing up in human form to relay the message of the Course in a way we can accept and understand. The Holy Spirit can show up as Jesus, an Angel, the Virgin Mary, or any other figure that inspires us. The form is not what matters; it's the content of the message. So whether or not you believe in figures appearing doesn't matter. The message of the Holy Spirit is brought to you in many different ways. Anytime you feel a sense of pure joy and excitement about something, or are attracted to certain people, places, or ideas, it is also a sign to pay attention. There is a reason you are feeling that excitement. Don't be afraid to act on it. The Course isn't against taking action. When it talks about being passive it means being passive to the ego, not the world itself. Let all your images be transformed to reflect your holiness, and you will know God.

Remember, the forgiveness steps are the same no matter what the situation appears to be. Many people feel they aren't doing forgiveness right because they don't feel peaceful, or nothing changes in their outer world. If you are shifting your thinking to reflect forgiveness as taught in the Course, and accepting the Atonement for yourself, you are doing forgiveness right. The outside picture doesn't always change, but that is not the point. The important thing is that your mind is being healed whether you know it or not yet. You will become more peaceful as you gracefully allow the process to unfold without any expectations of the outcome. Try and let it happen naturally. We all tend to move fast sometimes and want our enlightenment now. However, you can be in such a state of joy that the timing of your awakening from the dream doesn't matter. If there is a sense of urgency in awakening, that is also making the world real. So, as a line in a Beastie Boys rap song says, "Let it flow, let yourself go, slow and low, that is the tempo."

Gary and me

I can't think of a better way to end this chapter and book than by sharing a little bit about Gary and me, and our relationship. I haven't said too much about my relationship with Gary up to this point. But he just reminded me I wanted to talk a little bit about it when he came into the room while I was writing. "Cindy," he said, "I want to tell you something: I want you to know that every time I see you it makes me happy. It doesn't matter whether you are coming in from doing the laundry, running errands, or even walking into the room I'm in from another room…I am happy when I see you." At the beginning of our relationship he said, "There is nothing I wouldn't give you if you asked; anything. Just ask." So I asked him for a car (just kidding). But seriously, it was the *love* in which he said these things that was meaningful to me, not the "getting" of anything specific. Gary is a kind man, and what you see is what you get. I love that he is himself, and he is not trying to be some kind of guru. He is one of many powerful messengers of the bringers of truth. He is funny, witty and smart. He can make me laugh with one look or word. I've always felt that our bond goes very deep, and I knew that I had known him before when I first met him. It was an instant familiarity. He felt the same when meeting me. The connection was instantaneous.

All of this beauty doesn't mean we don't have our forgiveness lessons; we do. We don't always see "eye to eye" but that doesn't matter. What matters to me is how I feel when I am with him. Also, in the bigger picture of our relationship we know how to forgive. If there are upsets, it doesn't last long. It's over in minutes. At the end of the day, we always remember who the other is: Perfect Spirit, whole and innocent. I'm the kind of person that doesn't like to go to bed at night and bring a grievance with me. Not my style. Gary is the same. We share a lot of interests, including our love for music, movies, nature and animals, and of course…Hawaii. I think I love Hawaii just as much as Gary does. The three states where I feel most at home or have a resonance with are California, Colorado, and Hawaii. We've had amazing experiences in all three states, and more recently, Wyoming. This doesn't mean we don't love and enjoy the beauty of all the places we get to visit. We have seen the world. We are grateful for all the people we have met, and have heard their stories of joy and some of pain, but we are grateful for the thousands of people we have crossed paths with, all equally purposeful.

Sometimes we sit together and talk about all the places we've visited and done workshops. I couldn't ask for a better job. Every day we are grateful for all the people who read our books and share their experiences with us. It truly brings joy to our hearts. So we thank you. On days when we don't travel, I have a continuing counseling practice, where I help people apply the Course in their everyday lives. I truly enjoy that, too, and connecting with so many people around the world. We also have our online classes every month, teaching from different sections in the Course. I also like to write, and actually find the writing process very meditative. I feel the Holy Spirit with me when I'm writing, and it's comforting. I also like to read the Course, hike in nature, sing songs and write music, play with our cat, Luna, drink green tea, and eat my dark chocolate. Gary has the things he likes. We don't have to like the same things all the time. Sometimes he will be in the mood for a certain movie, and it may not be my style, so we can do our separate things and be okay with that. We don't always do everything (socially) together either. I have my time, and he has his, and then we come together. Love doesn't possess or own another. It frees the other to be as they are. I do know one thing for sure…I love Gary unconditionally, and as we often say to each other, *Love forever and forever in love.*

As you continue your journey with the Course, or whatever path you have chosen as the path that leads you to your true nature as love, remember that you are Holy even if you don't believe that yet. Remember, you can be in the business of forgiveness, by being kind and patient with yourself and others even in the midst of difficult circumstances. Smile more frequently. Laugh often. Remember you are loved beyond your wildest imagination. If you are ever uncertain or fearful about the road ahead, think of these words from Jesus in the Course:

In joyous welcome is my hand outstretched to every brother who would join with me in reaching past temptation, and who looks with fixed determination toward the light that shines beyond in perfect constancy.[12]

To the extent that you accept the light, to that extent you are healed. May your journey home be filled with wonder, joy, and the peace of God in the recognition you are always with Him in the reality of love.

Page for Personal Notes

ABOUT THE AUTHOR

Cindy Lora-Renard is an international speaker on *A Course in Miracles*, author of *A Course in Health and Well-Being*, as well as a spiritual life coach, with a Master's Degree in Spiritual Psychology from the University of Santa Monica. She has been traveling the world with her husband, Gary R. Renard, in addition to her solo events, helping to introduce the teachings of *A Course in Miracles* to many countries. Her first book is now in 5 languages. Cindy participates in the workshops through speaking, singing and guiding meditations.

Cindy is also an accomplished singer/songwriter. In her music, she blends an eclectic mix of New Age, and Alternative Pop with a Celtic flavor, as well as meditative sounds to create a unique style. Cindy uses her knowledge of *A Course in Miracles*, as well as in music and psychology, as "healing" tools to help others awaken into the "higher" octaves of life.

Cindy was born in Toledo, Ohio, to two very educated and accomplished teachers. Her father, Ron Lora (now in retirement) is an award winning History professor who taught at the University of Toledo in Ohio. Her mother, Doris Lora (now in retirement) was a highly respected Music professor at the same University, who later changed careers and received her Ph.D in Psychology. Both continue to remain very active in their communities.

When Cindy was 17 she moved out to Los Angeles, CA. with her mother where she still resides. She started on a spiritual path in her early 20's, going through the spiritual buffet line until she encountered *A Course in Miracles*, which became her chosen path. She eventually met and fell in love with her husband, Gary Renard, also a prominent teacher of *A Course in Miracles*, and best-selling author of several books of his own. A gradual process unfolded where Cindy realized the direction her path was meant to take. She continues to enjoy her work as a writer, speaker, spiritual life coach, and singer, and meeting people from all over the world. She likes to say, "We are all in this together."

KEY TO REFERENCES

As a key to footnotes and references, please follow the examples below of the numbering system used for *A Course in Miracles*. Other resources quoted from are also noted below.

T-26.IV.4:7. = Text, Chapter 26, Section IV, Paragraph 4, Sentence 7.

W-pI.169.5:2. = Workbook, Part 1, Lesson 169, Paragraph 5, Sentence 2.

M-13.3:2. = Manual, Question 13, Paragraph 3, Sentence 2.

C-6.4:6 = Clarification of Terms, Term 6, Paragraph 4, Sentence 6.

P-2.VI.5:1. = Psychotherapy, Chapter 2, Section 6, Paragraph 5, Sentence 1.

S-1.V.4:3. = Song of Prayer, Chapter 1, Section 5, Paragraph 4, Sentence 3.

In. = Intro.

YIR.Ch.2. P. 9 = Your Immortal Reality: How to Break the Cycle of Birth and Death by Gary. R. Renard, Chapter 2, Page 9

DU.Ch.7.P.365 = The Disappearance of the Universe by Gary R. Renard, Chapter 7, Page 365

AFF.Ch.4.P.10 = Absence From Felicity by Kenneth Wapnick, Chapter 4, Page 10

ENDNOTES

1. **An Introduction to Pure Non-Dualism**. 1. Preface.What It Says.Para.2. 2. Preface.What It Says.Para.1 3. Oxford Dictionary Definition 4. T-18. II.5:12-15 5. T-4.II.11:8-12 6. T-27.VIII.6:2-5 7. W-p1.132.6:2-5 8. T-26.V.3:3-6 9. T-13.I.3:5-7 10. T-13.in.2:5-6 11. T-23.II.18:8 12. T-13.in.2:2 13. M-14.1:2-3

2. **True Forgiveness vs. Forgiveness to Destroy.** 1. S-2.I.6:1-2 2. T-2.IV.3:10-13 3. T-21.VIII.1:1-2 4. S-2.I.3:8 5. S-2.I.5:1-4 6. W-p1.134.7:1-5 7. W-p1.23.5:2 8. W-p1.189.7:1-5 9. W-p1.189.8:7 10. S-2.II.6:2 11. T-22.III.6:5-8 12. T-2.VI.4:1-6 13. W-p1.134.17:1-5 14. T-18.IX.10:4-7

3. **Using Your Everyday Life As a Classroom.** 1. T-2.II.5:1-3 2. T-1.I.1:1-3 3. T-23.II.2:3 4. M-11.3:8-9 5. M-11.4:1-5 6. T-9.VII.1:6-8 7. T-9. VII.3:5-8 8. T-17.III.1:1-3 9. T-27.VIII.6:5 10. T-1.II.3:10-12

4. **Depression and Suicide: Stories of Survival and Working Through Mental Pain.** 1. W-p1.190.6:1-4 2. T-9.III.3:1 3. T-12.I.1:3 4. T-12. III.6:1-7 5. T-9.VII.3:5 6. T-12.III.9:2 7. T-12.III.9:8-10 8. T-21. VII.5:11-14 9. W-p1.31 10. T-21.II.2:1-5 11. W-p1.182.3:3-7 12. W-p1.47 13. W-p1.41 14. W-p1.137 15. W-p1.162 16. W-p1.50 17. T-4.I.7:2 18. T-13.X 19. T-5.IV.8:2 20. T-31.VIII 21. S-3.II.1:8-11 22. S-3.II.2:1 23. M-12.5:1-7

5. **Flip Your Script.** 1. Preface.What it Says.Para.5 2. T-8.I.2:1-6 3. T-8.I.3:1-3 4. DU.Ch.7.P.256 5. T-27.VIII.10:1-6 6. T-30.I 7. T-18. VI.1:1-2 8. T-18.VI.1:5-6 9. T-18.I.4:1-6 10. T-18.1.5:1-6 11. T-18.I.6:1-9 12. T-18.I.7:1-4 13. W-p1.193 14. W-p1.193.13:1-3 15. W-p1.193.13:4-7 16. W-p1.110.6:2-4 17. W-p1.72.9:1-2 18. W-p1.169

6. **Relationships For the Purpose of Healing: Special vs. Holy.** 1. T-15.V.8:1 2. T-17.V.6:6-8 3. T-18.V.6:1-2 4. T-18.V.7:1-6 5. T-15. VII.3:1-5 6. T-15.IX.2:3-6 7. T-15.V.1:3-7 8. W-p1.7 9. T-17.III.6:1-4

RESOURCES ON SUICIDE PREVENTION

1. National Suicide Prevention Lifeline: 1-800-273-8255

2. Child Mind Institute - An independent nonprofit dedicated to transforming the lives of children & families struggling with mental health & learning disorders.

    Website: https://www.instagram.com/childmindinstitute/?utm_source=ig_embed

SUGGESTED READINGS AND RESOURCES ON *A COURSE IN MIRACLES*

1. *"A Course in Miracles," 3rd Edition,* published by The Foundation for Inner Peace
2. *"The Disappearance of the Universe"* by Gary R. Renard
3. *"Your Immortal Reality: How to Break the Cycle of Birth and Death"* by Gary R. Renard
4. *"Love Has Forgotten No One"* by Gary R. Renard
5. *"The Lifetimes When Jesus and Buddha Knew Each Other: A History of Mighty Companions"* by Gary R. Renard
6. *"A Course in Health and Well-Being"* by Cindy Lora-Renard
7. *"All Peace, No Pieces"* by Jackie Lora-Jones
8. *"The Most Commonly Asked Questions About A Course in Miracles"* by Gloria and Kenneth Wapnick, Ph.D.
9. *"Absence From Felicity"* by Kenneth Wapnick, Ph.D
10. *"Healing the Unhealed Mind"* by Kenneth Wapnick, Ph.D.
11. *"A Vast Illusion"* by Kenneth Wapnick, Ph.D
12. *"Journey without Distance"* by Robert Skutch
13. Online classes with Gary and Cindy Renard on *A Course in Miracles*: To subscribe to the classes, please go to www.cindylora.com for more info.
14. For private, one hour sessions with Cindy over the phone or Skype, please contact Cindy through her website at www.cindylora.com

Also, please see Cindy's website for more information on how to contact her for booking an appearance, a private counseling session as well as ordering from her list of products.

Other books by Cindy Lora-Renard:

A Course in Health and Well-Being

Music and Meditation CD's:

Journey through Sound
Awakening to Love
Near the Beginning
Summer and Smoke
Meditations for Couples

THE FOUNDATION
FOR INNER PEACE

To learn more about *A Course in Miracles*, I recommend you visit the website of the authorized publisher and copyright holder of the *Course*, the Foundation for Inner Peace: www.acim.org. While there are many excellent organizations supporting study of *A Course in Miracles*, this is the original one with the greatest variety and depth of Course-related materials, including biographies and photos of the scribes, DVDs, free access to daily Lessons, audio recordings, information about the many languages into which the *Course* has been translated, and electronic versions of the *Course*, including mobile device apps.

The Foundation for Inner Peace is a non-profit organization dedicated to uplifting humanity through *A Course in Miracles*. The organization depends on donations and is currently immersed in translating the *Course* into many languages (26 to date). The Foundation also donates thousands of copies of the *Course*. If you would like to support more people to benefit from *A Course in Miracles*, donating to the Foundation for Inner Peace or one of the many other fine *Course*-related organizations would be a worthy endeavor.

Made in the USA
Las Vegas, NV
03 April 2024

88186727R00134